Sew a Work
of Art
Inside and Out

Charlotte Soeters Bird

That
Patchwork
Place®

Dedication

To Wallace A. Cole and Roberta Kopenberg, who commissioned my first garments in 1987. Little did they know how far I would go.

Acknowledgments

Writing this book has been a marvelous journey. I have discovered words for the art I make, and I have rediscovered the people in my life who have influenced the words and the art. As to the influential people, thanks to each of them for being available:

Laure Freudenberger Carlisle, a good friend who unwittingly provided the venue for my serendipitous meeting with Barbara Weiland and Nancy J. Martin from That Patchwork Place. They saw something in my work worthy of publishing, and Laure was the first to say, "You are going to do this, aren't you?"

Donna Joslyn, Elsa Saxod, Linda Torgersen, and the gang at The Studio, who are always available to help me work through my ideas until they look and sound right.

My mother, Dorothy Soeters, my grandmother, Alva Soeters, my great grandmother, Maude Reed, and my mother-in-law, Elizabeth Bird. These talented women taught me much about creativity, technique, and style, and each in her own way is a part of this book. I am sad that Alva and Elizabeth did not live to see the project finished. They were excited about it and gave me tremendous encouragement.

Special thanks to my husband and best friend, Charles Bird. He's always there saying "Go for it" when my inner voice is busy saying "It can't be done." We make a great team.

Library of Congress Cataloging-in Publication Data

Bird, Charlotte,
    Sew a work of art inside and out / Charlotte Bird.
      p. cm.
    Includes bibliographical references.
    ISBN 1-56477-172-5
    1. Vests. 2. Wearable art. 3. Patchwork. I. Title.
TT615.B56 1996
746.9'2—dc20   96-31340
                      CIP

Credits

Editor-in-Chief . . . . Kerry I. Hoffman
Technical Editor . . . . Barbara Weiland
Managing Editor . . . . Judy Petry
Design Director . . . . .Cheryl Stevenson
Copy Editor . . . . Tina Cook
Proofreader . . . . Melissa Riesland
Text and Cover Designer . . . . Cheryl Stevenson
Illustrators . . . . Carolyn Kraft, Bruce Stout
Photographer . . . . Brent Kane

Sew a Work of Art Inside and Out
©1996 by Charlotte Bird

That Patchwork Place, Inc.
PO Box 118
Bothell, WA 98041-0118 USA

Printed in Hong Kong
01 00 99 98 97 96   6 5 4 3 2 1

MISSION STATEMENT

WE ARE DEDICATED TO PROVIDING QUALITY PRODUCTS AND SERVICES THAT INSPIRE CREATIVITY. *We work together to enrich the lives we touch.*

Table of Contents

Introduction

    I have been sewing my own clothes since I was a child. My mother and I spent hours together at the end of each summer poring over the back-to-school *Seventeen* magazine, deciding how my look had changed and what I had outgrown. The look I grew most comfortable wearing was a bit unconventional, but not outrageous. I've always wanted people to say, "She looks great," not "Boy, what is that getup she's wearing?" That's what we were looking for each summer as I prepared my back-to-school wardrobe. And that's what I have carried into my adult life.

    I am a crafts person with my own business, Birdworks. I design and make one-of-a-kind women's clothing, including jackets, coats, and vests, that I sell at juried craft shows around the country. My business has given me the opportunity to see a lot of the United States and to talk to a lot of interesting and delightful people. Most important—for this book at least—it has given me the chance to try the shapes and color combinations I now use in the clothing I design. I am delighted to have the opportunity to share some of my designs and techniques for creating artwear.

    This book is about the adventure of creating a vest that makes a unique statement about you, the maker. It is about the process of creating as much as it is a guide for creating specific projects. It is about stretching—a little or a lot—to try something new and a bit risky. It is about having a stern talk with that inner voice that says, "Oh, no, it won't work. I could never wear something like that."

    As you will see in the following pages, I use strong color and texture combinations. I am most interested in abstract patterns and designs that I borrow from traditional quilting patterns and piecework techniques. I use these techniques in nontraditional ways, combining designs and colors to create a new, individual piece of cloth. Then, using basic garment shapes, I use the new fabric to design and construct a unique garment. To make this creative process possible, I collect and use interesting fabrics from around the world and from my favorite dressmaker and quilt fabric stores.

To put my signature on the resulting garment, I hand stamp or stencil the lining. First, I make the outer garment shell. Then I cut out the lining pieces and let the fabrics, shapes, and colors in the garment tell me what designs to use to embellish the lining. The lining adds a finishing touch, something to flash a bit, if you wish, or to enjoy just because you know it's there, like wearing a pretty lace slip. You can even wear my garments inside out for a wardrobe refresher and occasional change of pace.

Oscar Wilde once said, "If you cannot be a work of art, wear a work of art." I think everyone is a work of art, but it can't hurt to create and wear a work of art too. Use artwear as personal advertising to celebrate your individuality and uniqueness in the world.

The garments shown in this book include two vest styles. The Weskit is short and casual, while the Statement Vest is a bit longer, more like a sleeveless jacket. Although I use the techniques in this book on a variety of garment styles, I chose vests for the projects because they are easy and quick to make, and they provide a perfect medium for personal expression. Vests are fun to pop over other pieces in your closet for a finishing touch; they're great wardrobe extenders. Because you don't have to invest much time or money to make a vest, you'll find it easier to try a new technique, work with a new color combination, or execute an idea that's been incubating in the back of your mind for some time.

Many quilt books give directions for making a specific product using a particular quilt block or group of blocks. The size is set, the fabric requirements are given, and if the project is a clothing item, the block arrangement is also established. This book is a bit different, because I want to encourage you to take the next step—to put yourself into the project to make it unique. This book gives you a framework in which to work without dictating the results. To that end, I have provided directions for several garment shells and several possibilities for embellishing the lining. Choose those you like and want to try—the ones you will be comfortable wearing. Then your vest will reflect how you interpret the structure and vision provided in this book. As you work, remember that there is no one right way and no wrong way to sew a work of art.

Think of this as a mix-and-match book. You'll find a section on how to make several different vest fronts and another section on how to make several different vest backs. Combine your favorite front with your favorite back. The techniques will work for either the Weskit or the Statement Vest. Use my ideas and suggestions as a jumping-off point to explore and experiment with fabric and paint, with color and pattern, with line and design to create your own vision.

Each technique has a rating indicated by a star. The number of stars represents the degree of fearlessness required. The required technical sewing and painting steps are easily accomplished by a confident beginner. While sewing skill is important in creating a beautiful garment, making a snappy, exciting personal statement rests with the willingness to take risks and stretch to discover something new.

If you are a quilter, you have probably made sample quilt blocks and played with them on a design wall to see if you liked the emerging design. You have probably had some less-than-perfect results along the way that sent you back to your fabric stash and your sewing machine. Each time you go through a creative exercise, whether it succeeds or fails, you learn something valuable you can take to the next project. Before you begin a vest in this book, give yourself permission to enjoy the process. Remember, each project is practice for the next one.

So, sit back and browse through the pages of this book to examine your options. Then choose the techniques that are most appealing and the fabrics that make a statement—from quietly sophisticated to as wild as you wish—and go for it! I know you will be glad you did.

Charlotte Bird

PART I
Getting
Started

What is this vest going to look like? That's a good question. To answer, you need to decide where you want to wear it and what you want to wear it with that might already be in your closet. Decide on the mood you wish to set. What part of your personal style will it represent? Do you want a casual vest to wear with jeans, or something more sophisticated to add punch to your career wardrobe? What color palette will be most appealing—tone-on-tone, high contrast, monochromatic?

As you make these initial decisions, try not to burden the project with too many requirements. Ignore that critical inner voice: "It has to be perfectly made. It has to fit perfectly. It can't be too far out. I don't want people to laugh at me."

Our doubts, as Shakespeare wrote, are traitors and make us "lose the good we oft might win by fearing to attempt."

I keep a notebook-sketchbook with me all the time. It's small (at most 5½" x 8½") and has a pencil attached with a string. I use it to jot down ideas as they come to me—designs, doodles, thoughts. I add clippings from the newspaper, from magazines, from the junk mail that fills my mailbox each day. I also try to date the entry. It's fun and fascinating to look back through a full notebook to identify the beginnings of a current design or pattern in my work.

Very little in this world is totally original, so feel free to borrow and modify ideas to meet your needs and express your creativity.

Sewing Tools and Supplies

- Sewing machine in good working order with a new needle (size 12)
- Lots of pins (I prefer 1⅜"-long glass-head pins)
- Clear plastic rotary ruler with ¼" grid lines
- Fabric scissors
- Seam ripper
- Chalk pencil or marker
- Rotary cutter with new blade
- Self-healing rotary-cutting mat—the largest you can afford
- Seam sealant, such as FrayCheck™
- Pattern weights (I use rolls of 1"-wide masking tape; tuna fish cans also work.)
- Paper scissors
- Several sheets of poster board, each at least 20" x 30"
- Spray adhesive or gluestick
- Iron and ironing board or flat surface
- Freezer paper
- Four to six pieces of 30" x 40" foam-core board
- Value finder, such as the Ruby Beholder®

Embellishment Tools and Supplies

- Apron or old clothes
- Large plastic drop cloth
- Water container, such as a wide-mouth quart jar or large yogurt container
- Smooth, flat plates or trays for paint
- Water-soluble fabric paints
- Sheets of Mylar or lightweight clear plastic for stencils
- Craft knife with a new blade (#11)
- Household sponge with scrubbing surface on one side
- Assorted sponges and foam for painting
- Paper scissors
- Paper towels
- Several fine-tip plastic squeeze bottles
- Large hat pin or needle, to clear the gunk from the squeeze-bottle tips
- Several 1"-wide sponge brushes with wood or plastic handles
- Sponge dauber (See page 68.)
- Cotton-tip swabs
- Permanent markers with extra-fine tips for marking the stencil material
- Gold or silver fine-tip permanent fabric marker for signing your name on the lining

Planning Your Project

The project approach in this book is mix and match. You get to choose the garment, the fabric, the patchwork technique, and the lining-embellishment techniques you want to combine for your one-of-a-kind garment.

You have two pattern choices: the short (Weskit) or the long (Statement) vest. Or, adapt the techniques to a favorite commercial pattern. I suggest you use one of the patterns in this book for your first project, then move on to other designs. The following is a bird's-eye view of the process.

1. Decide which garment shape you want to make—the Weskit or the Statement Vest.
2. Select the correct size and prepare the pattern pieces (pages 9–11).
3. Select the fabrics and patchwork technique you want to use. Complete the fronts of your choice (pages 11–35).
4. Repeat step 3 for the back (pages 37–45). If you are making the Statement Vest, construct the collar and patchwork yokes (pages 55–57).
5. Make the vest shell (pages 57–59 and 62).
6. Cut out, embellish, and assemble the lining (pages 61–72).
7. Assemble the vest and lining, then finish the edges with bias binding (pages 73–75).

Pattern Selection

Most of us are not as tall or thin as the models in fashion magazines. Most of us have one or more figure features we would like to minimize or camouflage. You know what yours are, so keep them in mind as you make the design and color selections for your project. In addition, remember the following common-sense suggestions:

> Vertical lines are more flattering than horizontal lines on most figures.

> V shapes that draw the eyes from broad shoulders to a point on the upper half of the body are more flattering than a triangular design with the base at the hipline.

> V shapes with acute angles are more flattering than V shapes with wide angles.

More flattering

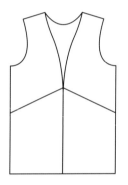

Less flattering

More flattering

Less flattering

Copies of the multisized patterns I used to make the vests in this book are included on the pullout. They are simple, basic shapes that are flattering on a variety of figures. Of course, you are free to use my ideas on other favorite patterns. For best results, choose a pattern that has no darts; no shaped, curved seams; and no collars that require neckline facings.

Avoid patterns with decorative seaming unless you want to embellish a whole section with patchwork piecing. The Statement Vest is a good example. The left front was originally made from two pieces. Then I realized I could piece the yoke shape and use it as an overlay on a complete vest front cut from fashion fabric. The result was a more professional-looking garment.

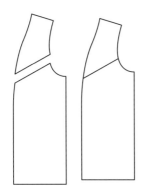

Original construction

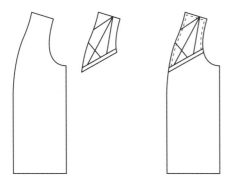

Pieced construction with yoke overlay

Cut the garment shell and the lining using the same pattern pieces. If your pattern includes separate lining and facing pattern pieces, you will not need them. I finish my vests with bias binding, so facings are not necessary.

Size Selection

The vests are made from basic shapes and are very loose fitting. When you select a size, think about the amount of ease you want. Refer to the measurements in the sizing charts below to select the correct size. (Note that the measurements given are the *finished* measurements of these roomy vests.) Choose a size that will hang straight from your shoulder and skim over your hipline. Your vest should also hang straight in front without overlapping, since there are no buttons or buttonholes. Make sure your pattern size has plenty of hip room. Your vest will not be comfortable or attractive if you must tug at it to keep it closed in front or to keep it from riding up on your hips. This is particularly important because you will be using cotton fabric for the lining, not a slippery fabric less likely to crawl up your body.

Weskit Finished Measurements

	Extra Small	Small	Medium	Large	Extra Large
Bust	38"	40"	43"	47"	51"
Back Neck to Hem	21"	21"	22"	22"	23"

Statement Vest Finished Measurements

	Small	Medium	Large
Bust	45½"	48½"	52"
Back Neck to Hem	31"	31"	31"

If you are uncertain what size to use, it's a good idea to make a test garment from muslin first. Choose the larger size for the test garment, and then adjust by taking deeper seams if necessary. It's better to cut a little large than to skimp on side-seam width.

Make any sizing adjustments to the pattern pieces before proceeding to the next step.

Pattern-Template Preparation

Since I construct the fabric for the vest fronts and some backs with patchwork piecing, I use the pattern pieces like templates as I cut and sew. I don't like to waste my precious fabric stash, so I construct the patchwork in relation to the pattern pieces rather than making a large piece of patchwork yardage only to cut a shape from it and throw away the rest.

I recommend gluing or tracing the pattern pieces onto poster board. If the back pattern piece is designed to be cut on the fold, trace a full back pattern. Trace around the first half, including the center back line, then flip the piece over and trace the second half. Or tape or glue the pattern piece in place if you prefer. If the fronts are reverse images, you need only one template. Label one side for the right front and the reverse for the left front. Transfer all pattern markings, such as notches and grain lines, to the template. If using one of my patterns, transfer the 60° lines as well. Cut out the templates, cutting small Vs at the notches.

If you are using a commercial pattern, use a protractor to mark a series of lines at a 60° angle to the lengthwise grain on the right and left front templates. Mark the same lines on the back, placing the protractor on the center back line.

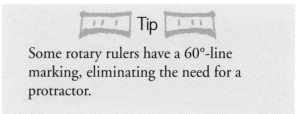

Tip

Some rotary rulers have a 60°-line marking, eliminating the need for a protractor.

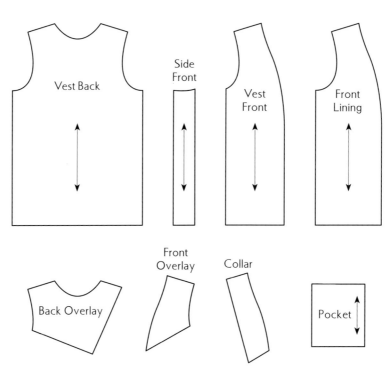

Pattern pieces for the Statement Vest

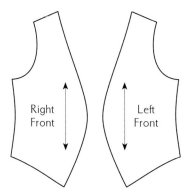

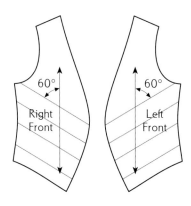

Pattern pieces for the Weskit

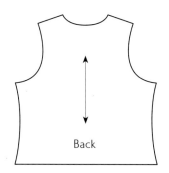

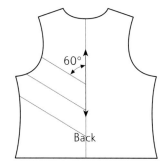

Pattern pieces for the Weskit
with 60° lines

Fabric Selection

Collecting fabrics for artwear is fun. Don't limit your search to quilt shops. Every now and then, wander through dressmaking and home-decorating fabric shops. When you travel, search out interesting fabric sources. Spend time in your local import store. You never know what you might find in the napkin department or among the bedspreads and tablecloths. (You will probably consider, then reject sheets, since they are tightly woven and difficult to sew.)

Of course, it is important to note fiber content and care requirements. Nonyardage fabrics such as tablecloths and napkins may represent a larger initial investment than a fat quarter (18" x 22" piece) or ¼-yard cut from your fabric store. Be sure you love it before you buy it, and be sure it is colorfast. Imported home-decorating items are notorious for bleeding and fading, since many have unstable dyes.

Use common sense. If the fabric has an odor, decide whether you want to take a chance and wash it. The odor may not come out. I tried washing a gorgeous tablecloth from India. It turned into a permanently wrinkled tablecloth with blotchy color—and it still smelled! Fortunately, I got a refund, but I had already spent my time and was disappointed. That's not to say that all imported items are risky. One season, I bought every crayon-bright Indian tablecloth I could find, and they worked beautifully.

In evaluating home-decorating items, remember that they often have stain-resistant finishes that do not wash out. Be sure you like their prewashed hand, just in case. Consider fabric weight too. Home-decorating fabrics are often heavier than quilting and dressmaking fabrics and may not be appropriate for your vest.

Color is one of the most important considerations when choosing fabric. Consider intensity, value, and pattern. Examine the garments shown in this book. Usually, I choose fabrics that are intense in color or of similar values or high contrast. When selecting prints, I use fabrics with overall patterns yet without recognizable elements. Geometric prints are especially nice, and I use lots of indigo and white, which are very Japanese in feeling. They are so restful, especially after I have been using lots of bright colors in my work.

Color theory is a scholarly study. Johannes Itten and Faber Birren made extensive studies of color. Their classic books are probably available at your library. Several authors have included basic theory in their books for quilters. I suggest reviewing *Designing Quilts: The Value of Value* by Suzanne Tessier Hammond (That Patchwork Place). It contains invaluable information on manipulating value in fabric combinations. Check your personal collection of quilt books for additional information on combining colors in patchwork, or ask for more information at the library.

Don't let color intimidate you. You already have a developed color sense that you use every day. I have no formal art training. Most of my color sense comes from practice and personal history. I use bright, full-intensity colors in part because my father is color blind. He can see those full-intensity colors, but has trouble with pastels. When I was a kid, we had the most wonderful hot pink bathroom with robin's-egg blue tile and red towels. We all loved it, and Dad could see and enjoy it too.

I call my method for choosing fabrics "controlled random selection." For most projects, I am interested in the overall look of the constructed patchwork fabric and how the patterns within it complement each other. I am usually not concerned about how each fabric looks by itself.

I use a few different techniques to select fabric. First, I use either a window or the bias-roll technique to see the fabric pattern.

To use a window:

1. Cut a 2" x 3" hole in an index card or heavy paper.
2. Move the card across the fabric surface, noting what you see and asking yourself these questions:
   ◇ Do the colors flow into each other?
   ◇ Are the transitions attractive when isolated?
   ◇ Is the pattern still identifiable, or is it more abstract? Shapes such as realistic (not stylized) flowers that continue to be identifiable through the window will be distracting in the finished garment because the eye goes immediately to recognizable shapes.

Since most of the projects in this book require strip widths of 1½" or 2", the 2" x 3" opening will give you an idea of what a fabric will look like when cut into strips. Refer to the photo below left.

When you don't have your window with you in the fabric store, use the bias-roll method. Fold the leading edge of the bolt on the bias, then roll the diagonal fold up or down, looking for the same characteristics you would with the window.

Fold on the bias to evaluate for patchwork.

Use a window to evaluate fabric for patchwork.

Next, I look at value. A red value finder, such as the Ruby Beholder (That Patchwork Place), is a wonderful tool for examining values in relationship to each other. Although it does not give accurate readings of red and red-related colors, it will help you see the value relationships of all other colors in a print. If you use a lot of red in your work (as I do), you might also want to have a transparent green, plastic report cover on hand (from an office-supply store) to check the reds.

Generally, I select fabrics with similar value readings. That does not mean that there is no value contrast within the printed design, but rather the overall value effect is close. I also use lots of prints that have black backgrounds or figures in the pattern. Black illuminates and adds a nice spark, especially to intense colors.

Fabric selection for garment projects is intensely personal. You can see which colors and patterns speak to me as you look at the garments in this book. Your taste may be entirely different and will surely show up in your garment if you wish to be comfortable wearing it.

You will need fabric for the garment shell—fashion fabric—and an assortment of fabrics for the patchwork. Begin by reviewing what is already available in your fabric collection. Keep in mind your personal style and the purpose of the vest you will be making. Pull out fabrics that appeal to you and stack them together. I throw my selections in a pile on a large table in my workroom. For any of the projects in this book, select at least twelve to fifteen fabrics in a close value range. Using that many fabrics offers enough variety to create a pleasing design.

After evaluating the fabrics you've selected from your stash, you may need to fill in with a few more. Fat quarters are ample if you are buying quilting cotton. Garment fabrics, however, are usually sold by the yard. Purchase at least ¼ yard of each to add to your group of fabrics.

Fold your fabrics neatly and stack, offsetting the folded edges so you can see all the fabrics in relationship to each other. Squint at the stack. If one of the fabrics sticks out, refold it and try again. There may be sections of it that don't work and sections that do. If the fabric still sticks out, replace it with something else. Otherwise, it will continue to overpower the other fabrics you have chosen.

For the garment shell, select a solid-colored fashion fabric, 44" wide or wider. Choose a color that blends with the piecework fabrics. My favorite for the garment shell is 100% silk noil. It has a smooth, almost cottony hand and a lightly slubbed texture. You can use any natural-fiber fabric of similar weight with a stable weave. I do not recommend fabrics with a high polyester content. They are difficult to handle and press.

Choose a solid-colored fabric, such as silk noil, for the garment shell.

Choose a variety of prints for the patchwork.

The Techniques

As I mentioned earlier, the techniques presented here are rated by level of fearlessness required, rather than by difficulty. You need only basic sewing skills and the willingness to take a chance. The techniques with two or more stars require a bit more fearlessness than the others only because there are more variables to keep track of as you cut and sew. For example, the Stack-and-Whack technique on pages 30–35 is difficult to visualize and requires both sewing skill and the ability to withhold judgment until you have completed all the sewing.

You will need to use a rotary cutter, mat, and ruler for some of the techniques. If you are skilled with these tools, read through the techniques in this chapter; then select the one(s) you wish to use, and get on with your project. If you have never used a rotary cutter, review "Rotary-Cutting Basics" before plunging in.

Rotary-Cutting Basics

You will need a rotary cutter and mat, plus a 6" or 8" Bias Square® cutting guide and a 6" x 24" acrylic ruler designed for rotary cutting. You can buy these tools at your local quilt shop.

1. Working on a rotary-cutting mat, fold the fabric in half lengthwise, aligning the selvages. Smooth out any wrinkles, working up and out from the fold toward the cut ends and selvages. There should be no wrinkles along the folded edge.

2. Place one edge of the Bias Square along the fold, then butt the rotary ruler against the edge of the square. The long lines on the cutting guide should be perpendicular to the folded edge, and the raw edges of the fabric should be under the ruler.

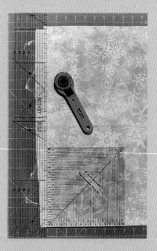

3. Remove the Bias Square. Place your hand on the ruler and press down to hold it firmly in place. Pressing firmly on the rotary cutter, roll it away from you along the ruler edge, from the fold to the selvages. This makes a clean-cut edge. Discard the trimmings.

4. Place the ruler on the fabric, adjusting so the clean-cut edge of the fabric is aligned with the correct measuring line for the strip width you are cutting. Cut along the ruler's edge with the rotary cutter. Be as accurate as possible to ensure straight, even strips.

5. If you need to cut the strips into smaller pieces, first square the ends, cutting off the selvages. Then place the strip horizontally on the mat with the ruler or Bias Square on top and the correct measuring line even with the short cut edge. Cut the required squares or rectangles.

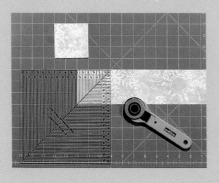

Preparing for Your Project

Before beginning, read through Parts II and III on pages 17–45 and select the techniques you will use to create your vest. Each section lists the required number of fabrics and yardages. Then follow these steps to get ready for fun.

1. Choose your pattern and size and adjust as needed. If you are using one of the patterns on the pullout, trace it onto tracing paper or pattern-tracing cloth, following the cutting lines for the correct size.

2. If necessary, make a test garment to adjust the pattern for your figure.

3. Mount the adjusted pattern on poster board as described in "Pattern-Template Preparation" on page 10.

4. Choose your fabrics, referring to "Fabric Selection" on pages 11–13. Look for fabrics that are similar in value. Make sure they blend well, with no one fabric overpowering the others.

5. Press each fabric to remove wrinkles, then square up with your rotary cutter.

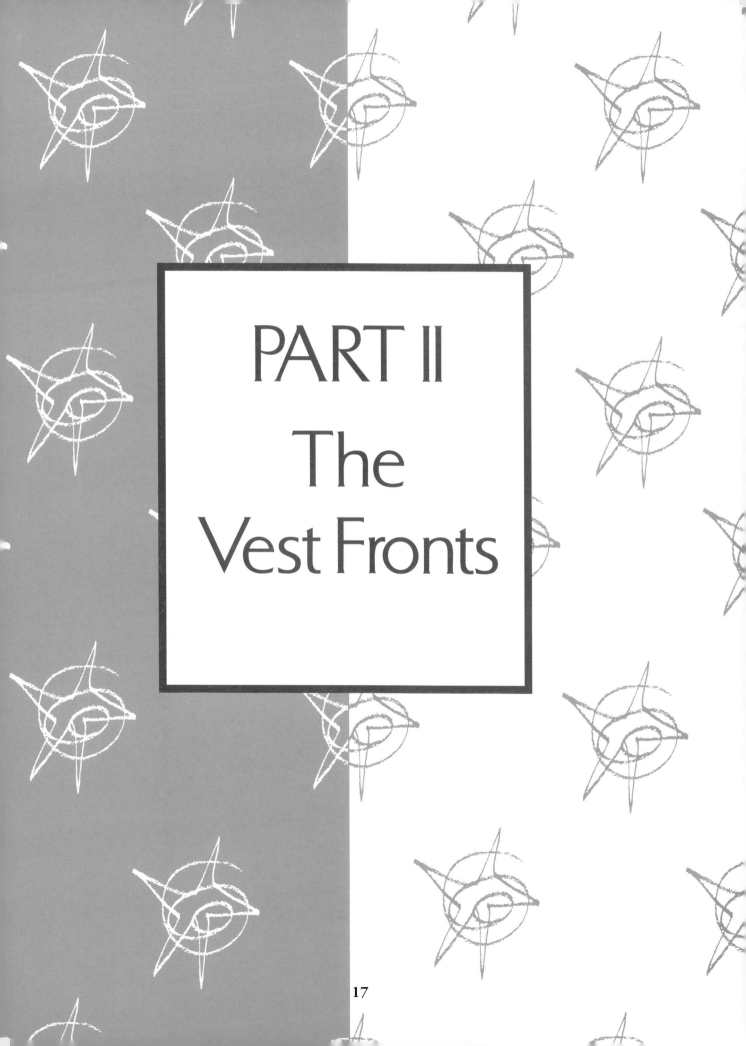

PART II
The
Vest Fronts

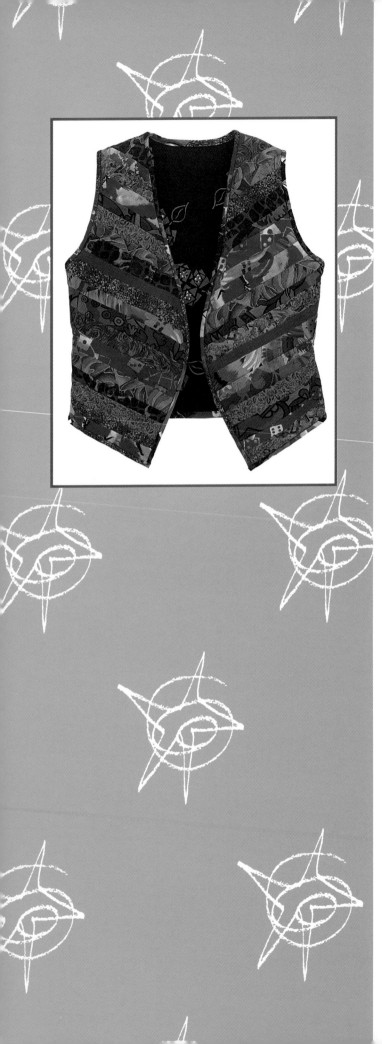

Strippy Vest Fronts ☆

This patchwork technique is the easiest, and the resulting vest is one you can wear for any occasion, depending on your fabric selections.

Materials

12 to 15 fat quarters (18" x 22") of coordinating fabrics*
Thread in a coordinating or neutral color
Weskit Front pattern pieces

If you plan to make the Braided Vest Back on page 41, you will need 2 fat quarters or ½ yard of each fabric. You will have extra fabric, but that allows for design flexibility while you work. Put the leftovers back into your stash for future projects.

Piecing

1. Complete steps 1–5 of "Preparing for Your Project" on page 15.
2. Using rotary-cutting equipment, cut 1 or 2 strips, each 1½" wide, and 1 or 2 strips, each 2" wide, from each of your fabrics. Cut all strips across the fabric width.
3. Using the right vest-front pattern template as a guide, arrange and sew strips together as desired, matching the 60°-angle lines and offsetting the strips as needed. The final piece of patchwork, referred to as a "blank" in the following directions, should be

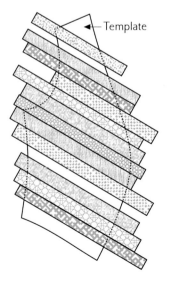

Template

slightly larger all around than the template. Use an accurate ¼"-wide seam allowance to sew the strips together, and press all seams toward the bottom edge of the vest front.

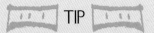 TIP

Don't think too hard about which strip goes next to which. Audition strips by laying them next to each other. Squint at them. As you do, you may discover that one or two of the fabrics really don't work after all. Set those strips aside and replace them with others.

4. Strip-piece the fabric for the left-front blank in the same manner, referring to the completed right-front blank so you are happy with the way the two fronts look together. Arrange the strips at a 60° angle that mirrors the right front. Don't try to make the left front a reverse image of the right, and be careful of placing the same fabric in roughly the same location on both fronts. It draws the viewer's eye to the similarity.

Cutting

1. After completing the strip assembly for the two front blanks, lay them on a large, flat surface so you can see if the design is balanced. You may need to remove and replace a strip or two to create a better balance in one or both blanks.

2. Place the pattern template for the right front on the strip-pieced blank, carefully aligning one of the 60° lines with a seam line on the blank. Place weights on the template and cut out the blank with your rotary cutter.

3. Chalk-mark all notches.
4. Reverse the template, then cut and mark the left front, using the remaining blank, in the same manner. Staystitch ⅛" from all raw edges on each vest front.

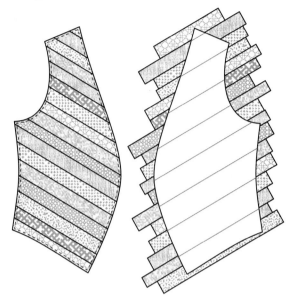

5. Set the fronts aside where you can see them, but where they won't get stretched or distorted. Remember, all the cut edges have some bias give; handle with care.

Moving On

Turn to "Part III: The Vest Backs" on pages 37–45 and follow the directions for making the back view you have selected. My favorites for this vest are the Plain Vest Back with Ties and the Braided Vest Back.

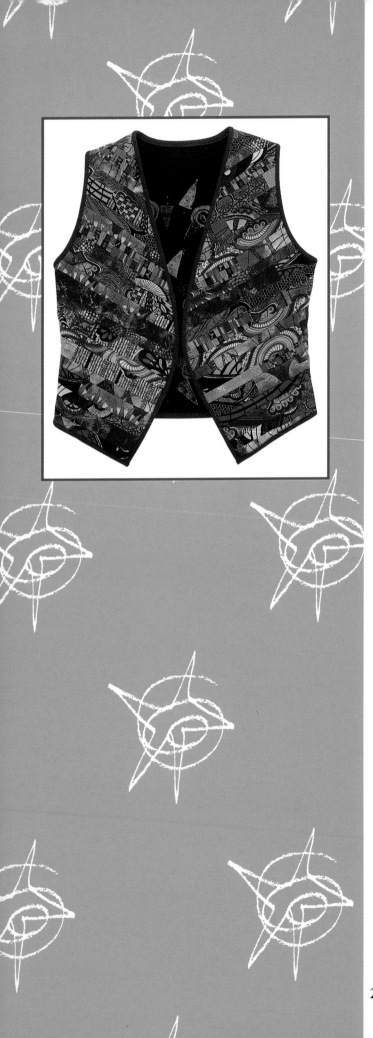

Strips and Strings Vest Fronts ☆☆

Strips and Strings is a bit more complex than the Strippy Vest Front, but the results are visually more interesting and the look slightly more sophisticated.

Materials

12 to 15 fat quarters (18" x 22") of coordinating fabrics*
Thread in a coordinating or neutral color
Weskit Front pattern pieces

If you plan to make the Braided Vest Back on page 41, you will need 2 fat quarters or ½ yard of each of your fabrics. You will have extra fabric, but that allows for design flexibility while you work. Put the leftovers back into your stash for future projects.

Piecing

1. Complete steps 1–5 of "Preparing for Your Project" on page 15.
2. For the most effective color and pattern play, select 5 to 7 fabrics from your grouping. From each of these, cut 2 strips, each 1½" wide, cutting across the fabric width. Cut 2 strips, each 2" wide, from the remaining fabrics. Keep the 1½"-wide strips and

the 2"-wide strips in separate piles. By using different fabrics in the two widths, you limit how often the same fabrics end up side by side in the garment fronts.

3. Working with each pile separately, cut each strip into lengths varying from 2" to 7".

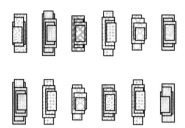

Cut strips into varying lengths.

4. Create the strings by arranging the pieces in any order that pleases you; then sew them together. Set your machine for no less than 12 stitches per inch. You will need a total of 8 yards of patchwork string in each of the two widths (1½" and 2"). You can sew all the pieces of each width together to make one long string, or you can sew pieces together in lengths that are several inches longer than the pattern width along the longest 60°-angle line.

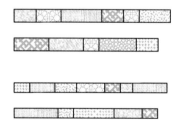

Join pieces in random order to make patchwork strings.

5. Press all seams in one direction. Carefully roll each string to make it easier to handle and to protect the short seams from separating while you work.

Arranging the Strings

1. Working on a large, flat surface, position a segment of either width along one of the 60° lines on the right-front pattern template. I usually start this process close to the center of the pattern piece and work out from there. This results in less distortion and fabric waste. Trim the string a few inches beyond each edge of the template.

2. Add a segment of the other string width above and below the first string. Continue alternating string widths to cover the pattern template. As you place the strings side by side, you will see patterns in seam location develop. Feel free to adjust the strings until the fabrics and seam placements are pleasing. If you don't like a sequence in a particular spot, set the offending string aside. You may find a place for it later.

3. Watch for places where the same fabric appears in about the same location a row or two away. In example A, the location of the irregular checkered fabric repeats two rows away. In example B, it has been shifted so it repeats in a different place.

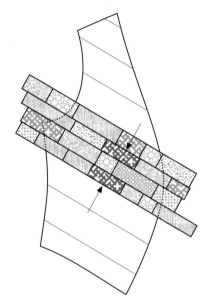

Example A

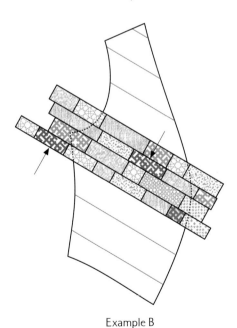

Example B

4. Sew the strings together, pressing all seams toward the bottom edge. It's easiest to position several strips on the template and then remove them one by one, sew them together, and press before laying out additional strings.

5. When you have pieced enough strings to completely cover the template, steam press the patchwork, referred to as a "blank" in the following directions.
6. Make the left front in the same manner, mirroring the 60° angle of the right front. Be careful to vary the string placement so it doesn't mirror the right front and so like fabrics don't end up directly across from each other. This encourages the viewer's eye to wander over the entire garment rather than lingering on the similarity of placement.

Cutting

1. After completing the string assembly for the two front blanks, lay them on a large flat surface so you can see if the design is balanced. You may find you need to remove and replace a string or two to create a better balance in one or both of the blanks.
2. Place the poster-board template for the right front on the blank for the right front, carefully aligning one of the 60° lines with a seam line in the blank. Place weights on the pattern template and cut out the blank with your rotary cutter.
3. Chalk-mark all notches.
4. Reverse the pattern template and cut and mark the left front from the remaining blank. Staystitch ⅛" from all raw edges of each vest front.
5. Set the fronts aside where you can see them, but where they won't get stretched or distorted. Remember, all the cut edges have some bias give.

Moving On

Turn to "Part III: The Vest Backs" on pages 37–45 and follow the directions for making the back view you have selected. My favorites for this vest are the Plain Vest Back with Ties and the Braided Vest Back.

Crazy Cabin Vest Fronts ✰✰✰

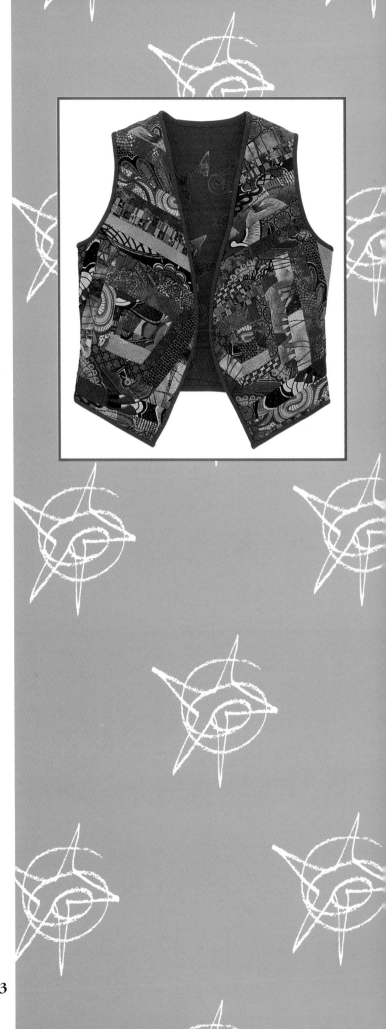

I refer to this as my Crazy Cabin vest because the construction is a variation of the traditional Log Cabin block.

Materials

12 to 15 fat quarters (18" x 22") of coordinating fabrics*
Thread in a coordinating or neutral color
Weskit Front pattern pieces

If you plan to make the Braided Vest Back on page 41, you will need 2 fat quarters or ½ yard of each fabric. You will have extra fabric, but that allows for design flexibility while you work. Put the leftovers back into your stash for future projects.

Piecing and Cutting

1. Complete steps 1–5 of "Preparing for Your Project" on page 15.
2. Using rotary-cutting equipment, cut each fat quarter into 1½"- and 2"-wide strips, cutting across the fabric width. When working with fat quarters, your strips will be 20" to 22" long. (If you are using standard ¼-yard cuts, cut 2 strips, each 1½" wide, and 2 strips, each 2" wide. The strips will be about 42" long.)
3. As you cut the strips, lay them side by side so you can see what is happening with the colors and patterns.

4. Cut 2 pieces, each approximately 2" x 2", from any of the 2"-wide strips. These are the Log Cabin centers. Your design will be more interesting if these pieces are not true squares.

Cut an off-square
for the center.

5. Select 1 strip of either width and sew it to one side of the center piece, using a ¼"-wide seam allowance. Press the seam away from the center piece. Trim the strip even with the center piece and press the seam toward piece 1.

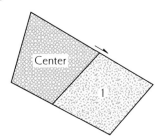

6. Rotate the unit a quarter turn, then add and trim the next strip in the same manner. Press the seam toward piece 2.

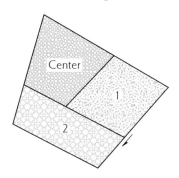

7. Continue adding strips until you have sewn 2 or 3 strips to each side of the center. Put a pin at the end of the last strip you add so that when you add more strips you will know where to start. You want to keep the rotation going in the same direction.

8. Place the unit on the right-front pattern template, aligning one edge of the patchwork unit with a 60°-angle line. Move the unit around, up and down, closer to the front edge, then farther away until you find a location that pleases you. This is a highly subjective process, but one location will definitely look better. Make a note on the pattern template about which fabric is located above the center piece in the position you like best.

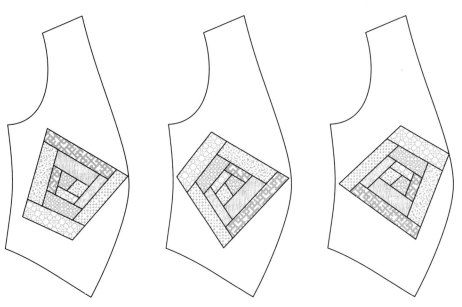

Rotate the patchwork on the template and choose the position you like best.

9. Continue adding strips around the unit until it covers the pattern template. When you have passed the side edges, fill in the bottom with additional strips, then the upper shoulder area, being careful to maintain a 60° angle.

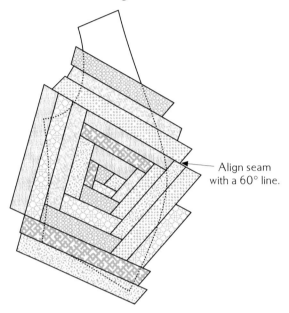

Align seam with a 60° line.

10. Press the completed patchwork, referred to as a "blank" in the following directions. I prefer to use steam when I press, but I am very careful not to pull or tug on the patchwork while it is damp.

11. Place the right-front pattern template on the completed blank, carefully aligning one of the 60° lines with a seam line in the blank. Place weights on the template and cut out the pattern piece with your rotary cutter. Use a chalk pencil to mark all notches.

12. Turn the pattern template over and repeat steps 5–11 to make the patchwork blank for the left front. Make it similar to the first, but do not make a mirror image. It is visually more interesting when the two fronts do not match. Keep the right front close to your work so you can refer to it often as you add strips to the left center piece. Stop occasionally to place the piece in progress next to the completed blank to compare. This will help you make strip

placement decisions. Press the completed blank and cut out the left front as you did the right, *using the reversed pattern template*. Staystitch ⅛" from all raw edges of each vest front. Take care not to stretch as you sew.

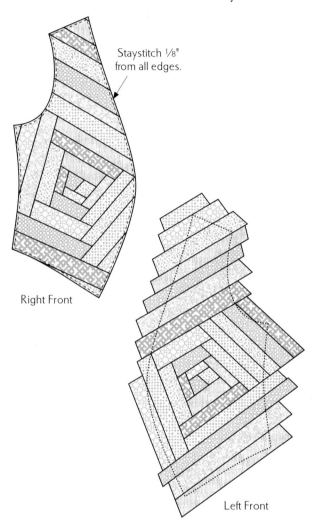

Staystitch ⅛" from all edges.

Right Front

Left Front

13. Set the fronts aside where you can see them, where they won't get stretched or distorted. Remember, all the cut edges have some bias give. Handle with care.

Moving On

Turn to "Part III: The Vest Backs" on pages 37–45 and follow the directions for making the back view you have selected. My favorites for this vest are the Plain Vest Back with Ties and the Braided Vest Back.

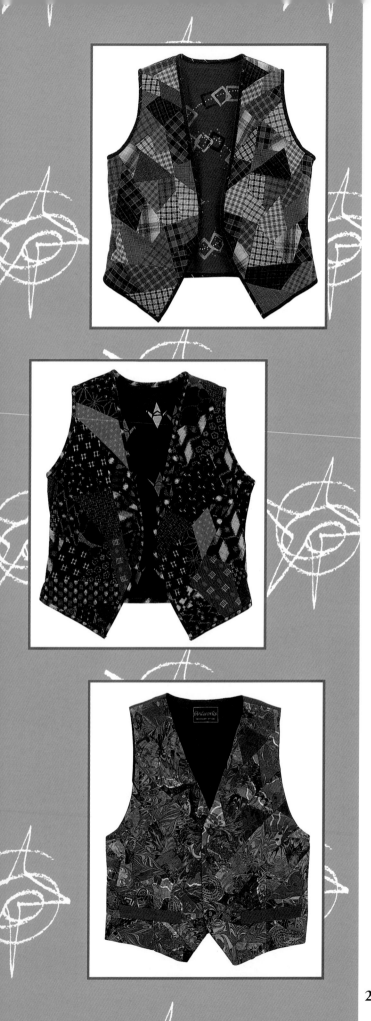

Crazy-Pieced Vest Fronts ☆☆☆☆

This relatively simple technique produces a sophisticated, complex-looking vest. It is a method Mia Rozmyn calls "polygonal piecing," and it works beautifully for clothing. For more information on Mia's techniques, refer to her book, *Freedom in Design* (That Patchwork Place).

I use twelve to fifteen fabrics for this technique. Review "Fabric Selection" on pages 11–13 before choosing your fabrics, and examine the vests shown. You can make these vest fronts completely different from each other, as I did with my blue vest, or you can make mirror-image fronts, like my plaid vest.

I love using Japanese yukata cloth for this vest. The similar backgrounds and print motifs blend beautifully. Muted plaids work well too. If you have difficulty choosing fabrics, look at your collection of fat-quarter bundles. They're already color coordinated!

Materials

12 to 15 fat quarters (18" x 22") of coordinating fabrics*
Thread in a coordinating or neutral color
Weskit Front pattern pieces

If you plan to complete this vest with the Crazy-Pieced Vest Back on page 43, you will need 2 fat quarters or ½ yard of each fabric. You will have extra fabric, but that allows for design flexibility while you work. Return the leftovers to your stash for future projects.

Preparing the Cartoon

To make each vest front, you need to prepare a full-scale pattern, or cartoon. You need 2 sheets of paper large enough to accommodate the vest-front pattern piece and 2 sheets of freezer paper the same size. You will use this to make freezer-paper templates for each design section of each front.

1. Complete steps 1–5 of "Preparing for Your Project" on page 15.
2. On the paper, trace around the poster board vest-front template, tracing 1 right front and 1 left front. Place the patterns side by side, front edges facing, on a large, flat working surface. These are your cartoons.
3. Using a pencil, draw lines and shapes to fill the pattern shape. Use geometric shapes or gentle curves as desired. Think about how you would sew the shapes together using a string-piecing method like the one used for "Strips and Strings" on pages 20–22. Avoid complex designs with lots of inset corners. Don't use shapes that have angles greater than 180°. Think "straight-line sewing."

This is a good time to draw two designs—one for the left front and one for the right. Hang them up together as if they were a garment and stand back to look at them. Squint. Do the shapes and patterns made by the lines form a pleasing overall pattern? Sometimes when I squint at a design, a secondary shape appears that has a broadening effect. I know this shape will be exaggerated when translated into color and pattern, so I know I need to adjust the design.

If you don't like what you see, tinker with lines. It's easier and less time-consuming to erase pencil lines now than to rip stitches later. Number each pattern piece in the sewing order.

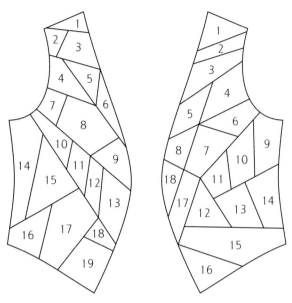

Each vest front is different.

Plan to sew segments together that can then be sewn to each other, using as many continuous or straight seams as possible.

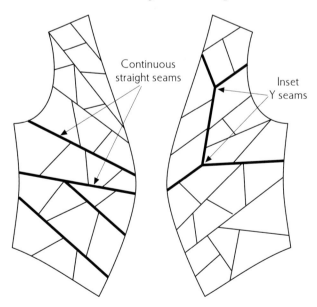

Continuous straight seams

Inset Y seams

The left side is easier to stitch. Each constructed unit can be sewn to the others with straight seams.

The right side has inset seams, where care must be taken. These Y-shaped corners can produce a pucker that is difficult to correct.

You may use a single design for both fronts as mirror images of each other. If you do, trace over the lines on the chosen design with a black pen, then flip it over, tape it to a window or light box, and trace the second front cartoon. To save paper, trace along the lines on the reverse side of the first design for a reversible cartoon.

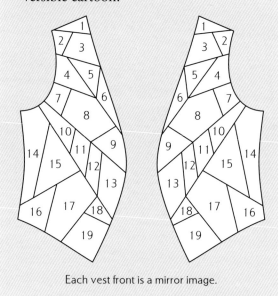

Each vest front is a mirror image.

4. If you haven't already done so, trace over the lines on each cartoon with a black pen or fine-tip marker.

5. Tape the cartoons to your work surface side by side. Cover each with a large piece of freezer paper, *coated side up*. Tape in place. Trace the shapes and the piecing design onto each sheet of freezer paper with a permanent black pen.

6. Remove the tape and turn the freezer-paper pattern over. Write the piecing-order numbers in the appropriate sections.

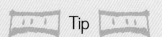

Tip

Use a different color ink for marking each front so you won't mix up the pieces.

7. Draw registration marks at various points along the design lines, particularly along curved lines. These are similar to the notches on garment pattern pieces. Make as many of these as you think you need based on your experience and tolerance for risk or error.

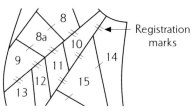

8. Using paper scissors, carefully cut out the numbered freezer-paper sections for each vest front. These are your templates. Arrange them on your work surface in numerical order.

Preparing the Fabric Pieces

1. Select a fabric for piece #1 on one of the vest fronts. Place the freezer-paper template *coated side down on the wrong side of the fabric* and press in place with a warm, dry iron. Cut the shape from the fabric, adding a generous ¼"- to ⅜"-wide seam allowance all around. Don't spend time making this an exact measurement. The generous seam allowances are particularly important on the pieces that touch the outer edges of the pattern. This ensures that the completed patchwork will be large enough to accommodate the pattern piece.

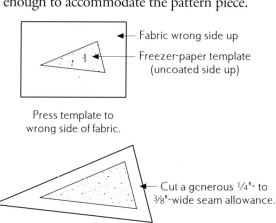

Press template to wrong side of fabric.

2. Cut and prepare all remaining pieces for each vest front in the same manner, repositioning them on the cartoon as you cut. Refer to the cartoon as you select each new

fabric to make sure you like the developing pattern and color composition. It's better to change your mind now, during the cutting stage, than to undo stitching later.

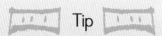

Tip

If you don't like a piece you've positioned on the cartoon, peel away the freezer paper and apply it to a different fabric. Freezer-paper templates can be used several times before they lose their stickiness.

Piecing

1. To join the first 2 pieces, place them right sides together. Each piece should have a freezer-paper template on the wrong side. Match the edges of the freezer paper at the ends by piercing the fabric with straight pins. Carefully line up the freezer-paper edges (not the fabric edges) and pin, with the pins perpendicular to the freezer-paper edge.

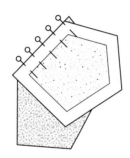

Align freezer-paper edges and pin.

2. Stitch along the freezer-paper edge 1 to 2 threads to the right of the template. Press the seam open and trim seam allowances to approximately ¼" where necessary.

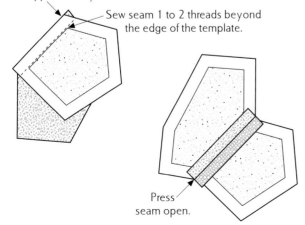

Trim to approximately ¼".

Sew seam 1 to 2 threads beyond the edge of the template.

Press seam open.

3. Continue adding pieces in numerical order until you have completed each vest front. The resulting patchwork blanks should be roughly the same size as your pattern piece—but a little larger all around if you cut generous seam allowances as recommended.

4. Remove the freezer-paper templates. Use tweezers to remove any paper caught in the stitching.

5. Steam press the completed patchwork blanks, being careful not to stretch them out of shape.

Cutting

1. Place the patchwork blanks face up on your rotary-cutting mat.

2. Place the poster-board pattern template on top of one blank and weight in place. Cut out the vest front with your rotary cutter. Mark notches with a chalk pencil.

3. Flip the pattern template on the remaining blank, cut out the remaining vest front, and mark the notches with a chalk pencil.

4. Set the vest fronts aside where you can see them while you prepare the back. Take care not to stretch the pieces out of shape.

Moving On

Turn to "Part III: The Vest Backs" on pages 37–45 and follow the directions for making the back view you have selected. My favorites for this vest are the Plain Vest Back with Ties and the Crazy-Pieced Vest Back.

Stack-and-Whack Vest Fronts ☆☆☆☆☆

This is the most complex of the construction techniques I use. It is also the riskiest and may require a little practice to develop confidence. I learned it from Nancy Crow and have adapted it for use in clothing.

The basic technique involves stacking several pieces of fabric and using a *sharp* rotary cutter to cut through all layers at once to create uneven strips or pieces in a variety of widths. These are rearranged, sewn together, then cut, rearranged, and sewn together again.

In experimenting with this technique and a variety of fabrics, I have discovered that using three to four solid-colored fabrics with one coordinating print produces appealing results. I prefer bright, intense colors for this method.

Since I make one-of-a-kind clothing to sell, I prefer silk noil for the solid-colored fabrics in this vest. Silk noil is a sophisticated but very wearable fabric that has most of the stability and sewing ease of cotton, in addition to possessing the prestige that appeals to my clients. If not available at your local fabric store, check "Mail-Order Sources" on page 78.

When you are ready to try this technique, clear a large work space. You need plenty of room to lay out the pieces as you sew the Stacked-and-Whacked sections together. If you select five fabrics for your vest, you will need space for five garment sections. This technique makes enough patchwork for two vest fronts and one vest back.

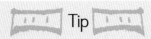
Materials

½ yd. each of 3 or 4 solid-colored fabrics
½ yd. of a coordinating print
Thread in a coordinating or neutral color
Weskit Front pattern pieces
4 or 5 sheets of foam-core board

Stacking and Whacking

1. Complete steps 1–5 of "Preparing for Your Project" on page 15.
2. Working on your rotary-cutting mat, stack the pressed fabric face up, smoothing out any wrinkles and aligning selvages. (Do not fold the fabrics in half; they should be open to their full width for layering.) Use your rotary-cutting equipment to cut off the selvages so all the pieces are the same size. (Some fabrics may be more or less than 44" wide.)

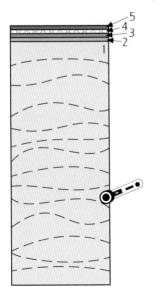

3. Put a fresh blade in your rotary cutter, then make several freehand cuts (5 or 6 is plenty) through all the layers, from selvage to selvage across the ½-yard length of the fabrics. Hold the rotary cutter so the blade is vertical, and hold the fabric with your other hand to reduce distortion caused by cutting. If you are working on a small cutting mat, you may need to cut a section, and then shift the fabric on the mat to complete the cuts. If so, be very careful not to pull at or cut into the cut edges. Vary the widths of the strips you cut. The finished work will be more interesting if the sizes and shapes of the cuts vary.

Combining the First Cuts

1. Beginning at one end of the fabric stacks, lay out each color on its own sheet of foam-core board in the same order it was cut. You need 1 board for each fabric in the stack.

2. Assign a number to each fabric and arrange them in new combinations, referring to the illustration below. Because the pieces were all cut at the same time, they will fit together like a puzzle. Rotate the colors by one until all the pieces have been placed. I have tried several different ways of rotating, and they all work fairly well. The color rotation shown, however, produces the most uniform combinations, which may be important to the look of the completed garment.

3. Take a deep breath, then sew each set of puzzle pieces together—without pinning, if you can. Use a ¼"-wide seam allowance. This takes practice, so relax and just begin.

   Gently hold the pieces, right sides together, using your fingers and thumb. I find holding the top fabric with my left hand and the bottom fabric with my right hand works well. Backstitch at the beginning, then sew at a reasonable (not slow) speed, holding the edges together for about 6" in front of the needle. When you reach your hands, reposition them along the remaining seam edge. Continue stitching and adjusting the layers until you reach the end. Backstitch to secure.

4. Sew each set together in the same manner, then place each patchwork unit right side up on your ironing board. Smooth it as flat as you can with your hands.

   Next, you are going to break all the rules you learned about pressing. With your steam iron set at the appropriate setting for your fabric, press the seams flat, allowing them to lie in whatever direction is best to accommodate the curves. Use lots of steam. If a seam won't lie flat, consider clipping it. If it is really stubborn, you may need to restitch part of the seam, then press again.

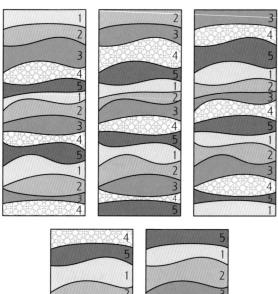

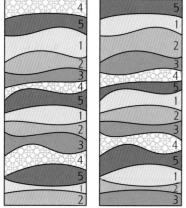

Color Rotation for Stack-and-Whack Vest Front

If you've stitched and restitched a seam (or a portion of one) and made a hole in the patchwork, you'll need to add a fabric patch. Use a different fabric for the patch so it looks like you did it on purpose.

Making and Combining the Second Cuts

1. Stack the pressed patchwork pieces in the following manner:

> Place 1 piece on another, both pieces face up and seam lines matching as closely as possible.

> Place the next 2 or 3 pieces face down, seam lines matching as closely as possible.

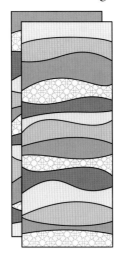 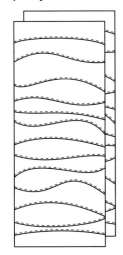

2 pieces face up on top of each other

Add 2 or 3 pieces face down on top of the first two.

 Note ▷

You cannot match the seam lines in the face-up units to those in the face-down units. Make sure the edges of the four or five pieces are as closely aligned as possible.

2. Look carefully at the vests on page 30. In all three, the predominate seam lines are at a 60° angle. Notice that the fabric pieces in two of the vests are almost diamond shaped. In the other vest, however, the fabric pieces are more rectilinear in shape. The second cuts for this vest were made roughly perpendicular to the seams, similar to the possibilities shown in the illustration below.

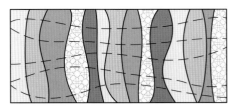

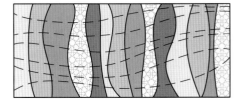

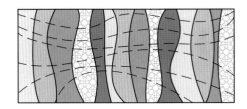

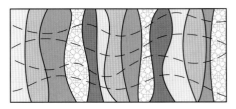

Examples of second cuts made perpendicular to the seams

The 60° angle was achieved by laying the pattern pieces on the patchwork fabric so the short side seams were at a 60° angle.

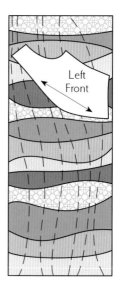 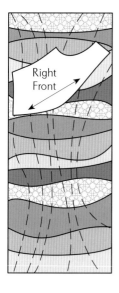

For a vest with shapes that are more diamond-like, start by placing a rotary ruler with a 60° line close to the fabric stack as a reference. Using your rotary cutter, make freehand cuts through all the fabric layers at a 60° angle. You will be cutting across layers of seam allowances, so bear down on the cutter while holding the fabric stack firmly in place with your other hand. Cut carefully and decisively to reduce distortion and drag on the fabric. In the illustration below, the 4 fabric layers have been placed side by side so you can see the results of this cutting method. Because these cuts are on the diagonal, there are many bias edges. Handle the pieces carefully to avoid distortion.

3. Recombine the second set of cuts into new arrangements as you did after making the first set of cuts. Combine the pieces that were cut face up. Do the same with the pieces that were cut face down. You should have 2 sets of mirror-image units plus an extra unit if you used a total of 5 fabrics. If you forgot to place some of the pieces face down, all the cuts will be at the same angle and all the seams will spiral in one direction around your body. Mirror-image cuts are much more flattering.

4. Sew the pieces together in each group, using the same technique used to sew the first cuts together. Match seams as best as you can as you sew the strips together. Exact matches are usually impossible because of the distortion that occurs during the cutting and freehand seaming. Handle the bias edges with care to prevent any further distortion.

5. Press each patchwork piece ruthlessly, with lots of steam. You may have to manipulate areas where seams intersect and make a bump. Flatten bumps as much as possible.

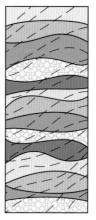   

Cutting

1. Arrange the completed patchwork blanks on your work surface and select mirror-image blanks for the vest fronts. Set the remaining blanks aside for the vest back.
2. Place one of the blanks on your cutting mat. Place the pattern template on top, aligning the 60°-angle line with the 60° seam lines. Weight the template.

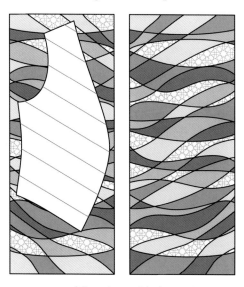

Mirror-image blanks

3. Cut around the pattern template with your rotary cutter. Chalk-mark all notches.
4. Flip the pattern template and place on the other patchwork blank. Weight and cut in the same manner. Set the remaining pieces of patchwork aside for the vest back or other projects.

Moving On

Turn to "Part III: The Vest Backs" on pages 37–45 and follow the directions for making the back view you have selected. My favorites for this vest are the Plain Vest Back with Ties and the Stack-and-Whack Vest Back.

PART III

The Vest Backs

The vest back can be fairly simple with an easy-to-make tie, or it can be pieced for a more complex look. If you're eager to finish your vest, choose one of the tie versions. If you're still enjoying the piecing, choose one of the patchwork backs and keep on stitching.

Plain Vest Back with Ties ☆

Materials

Approximately ¾ yd. solid-colored fabric that
    coordinates with the patchwork in your
    vest front*
Leftover fabric strips for the belt
Weskit Back pattern piece
Thread in a matching or neutral color

*I prefer silk noil, but there are many options, including 100% cotton or dressier woven fabrics made of natural fibers.

Preparing the Vest Back

1. Complete steps 1–5 of "Preparing for Your Project" on page 15 if you have not already done so.
2. Place the fabric on your cutting mat in a single layer. Place the poster-board Weskit Back pattern template on top and align the grain line with one of the selvages. Weight the template and cut out the piece with a rotary cutter. Chalk-mark all notches.
3. Using a rotary ruler and dressmaker's chalk, draw a line from side-seam notch to side-seam notch across the vest back. Measure the line and make a chalk mark at the center and another chalk mark 7" in from each side. This marks the tie position.

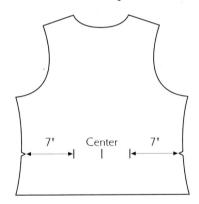

4. Choose and make your favorite back tie from the 3 that follow. Attach to the vest back as directed with each tie.
5. To complete your vest, refer to "Assembling the Vest" on page 62.

Simple Ties

1. From your fabric leftovers, select 2 strips, each 2" x 20" or longer. They can be matching or nonmatching fabrics. I often use a different fabric for each tie because it is more visually interesting, but you can use the same fabric for both ties if you prefer.
2. Fold each strip in half lengthwise, right sides together and raw edges even. Stitch ¼" from the raw edges. Turn the tubes right side out and press with the seam along one long edge.

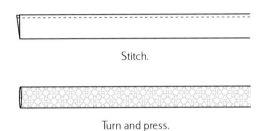

Stitch.

Turn and press.

3. Tie a tight overhand knot at 1 end of each tie, leaving a 1"-long tail. Manipulate the knot so the tail will lie flat. Trim the tail end at an angle and treat it with a light bead of seam sealant, such as FrayCheck. Allow to dry. For a more finished look, turn the raw edges in and edgestitch or slipstitch the edges together.

Apply seam sealant to prevent fraying.

4. Tie the two tubes together in a square knot, allowing for 3"- to 4"-long knotted tails.
5. Position the knotted ties on the vest back along the chalk line, with the square knot at the center mark. Pin in place along the chalk line and trim any excess tie at the side seams. Stitch 1 edge of each tie in place, ending the stitching at the chalk mark, then pivot, stitch across the tie width, pivot, and stitch close to the remaining edge.

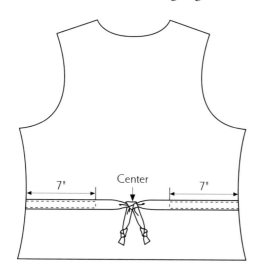

Pieced Ties

1. Cut or select several leftover 2"-wide strips and make 2 pieced strings, each 20" long.

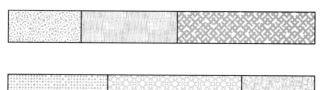

Make 2 strings, each 20" long.

2. Follow steps 2–5 above for "Simple Ties" to complete the ties and attach them to the vest back.

One-Piece Knotted Tie

1. From your fabric leftovers, select 2 strips, each 2" x 28". I often use a different fabric for each strip because it is more visually interesting, but you can use the same fabric if you prefer.
2. With right sides facing, stitch the 2 strips together, ¼" from each long edge. Turn right side out and press.

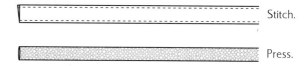

Stitch.

Press.

3. Tie a single overhand knot. If you used 2 different fabrics, manipulate the knot so one fabric shows to the right of the knot and the other shows to the left.
4. Place the knotted tie on the vest back with the knot at the center mark and the lower edge along the chalk line. Pin in place. Stitch close to each edge, pivoting at the chalk marks to anchor the tie to the vest as shown.

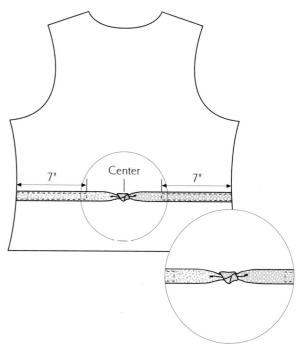

Braided Vest Back ☆☆☆

Materials

12 to 15 fat quarters (18" x 22") of the same
    fabrics you used for the vest front
Thread in a coordinating or neutral color
Weskit Back pattern piece

Piecing

1. Complete steps 1–5 of "Preparing for Your
   Project" on page 15 if you have not already
   done so.
2. Place the back pattern template on your
   work surface and draw a line down the center back.
3. From one of the fabrics, cut a 5"-tall equi-
   lateral triangle (60° angles).

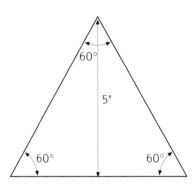

4. Using rotary-cutting equipment, cut 1 or 2
   strips, each 1½" wide, and 1 or 2 strips,
   each 2" wide, from each fabric. Cut all
   strips across the fabric width. Use any strips
   left over from the vest fronts too.

5. Select 1 of the strips and stitch it to 1 side of the triangle, using a ¼"-wide seam allowance. Press the seam away from the triangle.

6. Stitch a strip to the opposite side of the triangle in the same manner and press the seam away from the triangle.

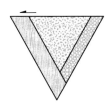

7. Continue adding strips, alternating from side to side and alternating strip widths. It is important to alternate strip widths on each side to prevent distortion along the braided center. Press each seam away from the triangle before adding the next. Periodically place the patchwork piece on top of the pattern template, aligning the braided center with the center back line to see if the piece is large enough to cut the back from it.

Cutting

1. Place the patchwork blank on your rotary-cutting mat.
2. Place the pattern template on top, making sure the center back line lies along the braided center line. Weight the template and cut out the pattern piece with your rotary cutter. Chalk-mark all notches.
3. Carefully staystitch ⅛" from all edges to prevent stretching.

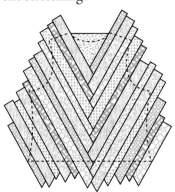

4. To finish your vest, refer to "Assembling the Vest" on page 62.

Crazy-Pieced Vest Back ☆☆☆☆☆

Materials

12 to 15 fat quarters (18" x 22") of the same
   fabrics you used for the vest front
Thread in a coordinating or neutral color
Weskit Back pattern piece

Piecing

1. Complete steps 1–5 of "Preparing for Your
   Project" on page 15 if you have not already
   done so.
2. Refer to "Crazy-Pieced Vest Fronts" on
   pages 26–29 to make a cartoon and to piece
   the blank for the vest back.

Cutting

1. Place the patchwork blank on your rotary-
   cutting mat.
2. Place the pattern template on top. Weight
   the template and cut out the piece with
   your rotary cutter. Chalk-mark all notches.
3. Carefully staystitch ⅛" from all edges to
   prevent stretching.

4. To finish your vest, refer to "Assembling the
   Vest" on page 62.

Stack-and-Whack Vest Back ☆☆☆☆☆

Materials

Stack-and-Whack patchwork units left over from
making the vest fronts (pages 30–35)
Thread in a coordinating or neutral color
Weskit Back pattern piece

Cutting

1. Prepare the poster board vest-back pattern
   template as directed on pages 10–11 if you
   have not already done so.
2. Choose 2 mirror-image units of Stack-and-
   Whack patchwork. Place them on your
   cutting board and use a rotary ruler with a
   60°-angle line to cut a straight edge on each
   patchwork unit.

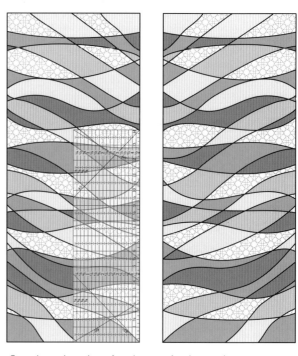

Straighten the edge of each piece for the vest's center seam.

44

3. With right sides facing, stitch the patchwork units together along the straight-cut
   edges, using a ⅜"-wide seam allowance.
   Press the seam open.

4. Place the patchwork blank on your rotary-
   cutting mat.

5. Place the pattern template on the blank,
   aligning the center line on the template
   with the center back seam line. Weight the
   template and cut out the pattern piece with
   your rotary cutter. Chalk-mark all notches.

6. Carefully staystitch ⅛" from all edges to
   prevent stretching.

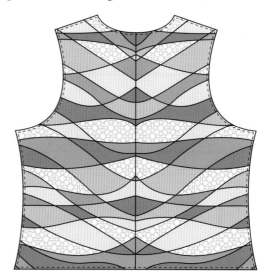

7. To complete your vest, refer to "Assembling
   the Vest" on page 62.

PART IV
The Kaleidoscope Vest

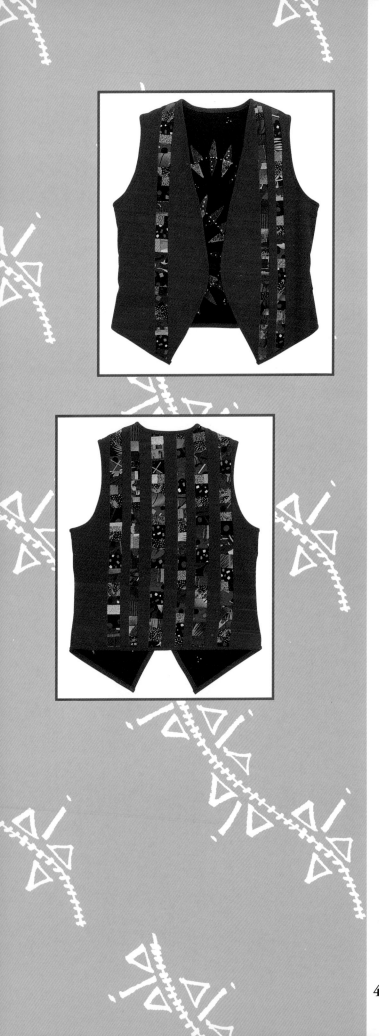

Kaleidoscope Vest ☆☆☆

This is a relatively simple vest to make, with a patchwork design that continues from front to back, unlike the mix-and-match vests in Part III. You can make it casual or dressy, depending on your fabric selections.

Materials: 44"-wide fabric

2½ yds. fashion fabric in a solid color for the vest piecing and binding*

12 to 15 fat quarters (18" x 22") or ¼ yd. each of coordinating prints

Thread in a coordinating or neutral color

Weskit pattern pieces

You may decide later to use a contrasting binding, but if you buy this much fabric now, you will be sure to have enough for a matching binding. Matching the fabric later may be impossible, since dye lots vary, particularly in silk noil. (For a contrasting binding, you will need ½ yd. of fabric.)

Cutting the Fashion Fabric

1. Complete steps 1–5 of "Preparing for Your Project" on page 15. Cut V-shaped notches at the top and bottom edges of the poster board vest-back pattern template to mark the center for easy placement of the patchwork blank. Do the same at the ends of the grainline marking on the front pattern template.

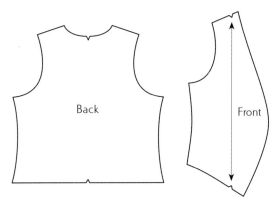

2. Cut a ½-yard length from the fashion fabric and set it aside for the binding.

3. Measure the length of the Weskit Front pattern template at its longest point and add 2". Then, measure across at its widest point and double that measurement for 2 fronts. Cut 1 piece of fashion fabric with these length and width measurements. Measure the Weskit Back pattern template across its length and width, adding 2" to the length. Cut 1 piece of fabric to these measurements.

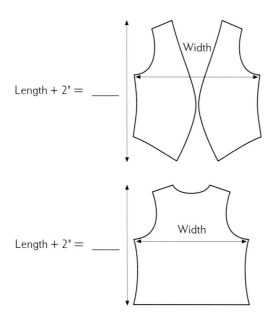

Length + 2" = _____

Width

Length + 2" = _____

Width

4. With the fashion fabric for the vest front on your cutting mat, cut the following strips as shown. Label the strips and set aside. (I use small, brightly colored sticky notes to label my piles of strips.)

4 strips, each 7" wide (If a single vest front is wider than 14", increase the strip width so 2 strips equal the width of the vest front.)

1 strip, 1½" wide

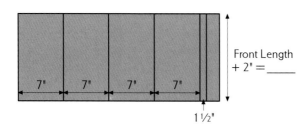

7"   7"   7"   7"

Front Length + 2" = _____

1½"

5. With the fashion fabric for the vest back on the cutting mat, cut the following strips as shown. Label the strips and set aside with the front strips.

2 strips, each 7" wide
2 or 3 strips, each 2" wide
2 or 3 strips, each 1½" wide

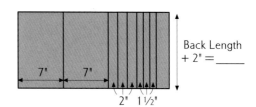

7"   7"

Back Length + 2" = _____

2"   1½"

Cutting the Print Fabrics

1. If you are using ¼-yard pieces instead of fat quarters, cut each piece in half to make 2 pieces, each 9" x 22".

2. Stack several pieces of fabric (no more than 5) on the cutting mat, and make a clean cut along one long edge. (Refer to "Rotary-Cutting Basics" on pages 14–15.) Then cut at least 2 strips, each 2" x 22", and 2 strips, each 1½" x 22", from each print.

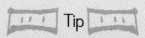 Tip

Don't try to hurry the cutting by layering more than 5 fabrics. The cutter bogs down in more layers and the cuts are not clean. It's actually faster and easier to cut through fewer layers. Make sure your blade is sharp.

3. Using a ¼"-wide seam allowance, stitch the strips together along the long edges, arranging them randomly to make 2 strip-pieced units, each approximately 18" x 22". Don't labor over the positioning of the strips. Part of the magic of this technique is the color and pattern juxtapositions created by the haphazard placement of the strips in each unit.

4. Press all seams in one direction.
5. Cut 1 strip-pieced unit into 2"-wide strings; cut the remaining unit into 1½"-wide strings.

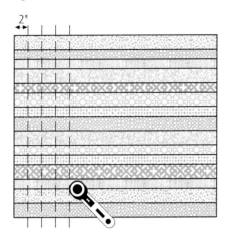

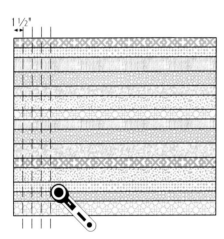

6. Sew the strings together, end to end, to make 2 long strings, 1 of each width. Roll up each string for easier handling. If you wish, roll the strings onto an empty paper-towel tube.

Piecing the Fronts

You will be making two vest fronts, but they will not be identical.

1. Place 2 of the 7"-wide strips of fashion fabric for the vest front on your cutting mat, side by side. Arrange the remaining 7"-wide strips for the front with the 1½"-wide strip between them.

2. Cut 1 piece of the 2"-wide string the length of the vest front and place it between 2 of the 7"-wide strips for 1 front. Cut 2 pieces of the 1½"-wide string the length of the vest front, making sure the fabric placement within each string varies. You may need to waste a bit of string in order to shift the fabric positions for a pleasing composition. Save those pieces. You can sew them to the end of the string if you find you need more length. Place the 1½"-wide piece of fashion fabric between the two strings, and then place this unit between two 7" pieces to make the second front.

3. Sew the strips together to make the blanks for the fronts. Press the seams toward the fashion fabric.

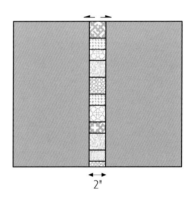

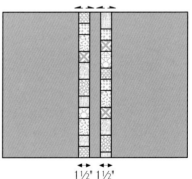

4. Set the front blanks aside, keeping them as flat as possible until you are ready to construct the vest.

Piecing the Backs

1. Arrange the back fashion-fabric strips on the cutting mat to the approximate width of the poster board vest-back pattern piece with the wider strips at the outer edges.

2. Cut lengths of the 2"- and 1½"-wide strings to place between the fashion-fabric strips. Use the strings in whatever order you wish, making sure to adjust so the prints are not in the same position across the back. (If fabrics line up, they create an obvious, undesirable line for the eye to follow *across* the back. You want the eye to move *up and down* the back.)

3. Sew the strips together to make the blank for the back. Press the seams toward the fashion fabric.

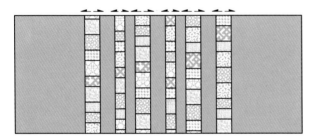

Cutting

1. Arrange the vest-front blanks on your cutting board and decide which will be the right front and which the left.

2. Place the vest-front pattern template on top of one of the front blanks and adjust so the template grain line aligns with one of the seam lines. Weight to hold it in place and cut out the vest front, using your rotary cutter. Chalk-mark all notches.

3. Flip the pattern template and cut and mark the second vest front from the remaining blank in the same manner. Staystitch ⅛" from the raw edges. Set the fronts aside on a

flat surface to reduce the risk of stretching the cut edges.

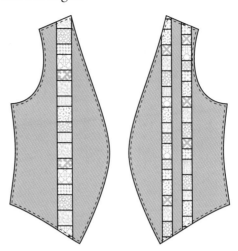

4. Place the vest-back blank on the cutting surface and adjust the vest-back pattern template so the center back line is aligned with a seam line and the blank is roughly centered under the template. If you place the strips off-center, the finished vest back will be disconcerting to the viewer. Make sure the distance from the shoulder at the armhole edge to the first pieced strip is the same on each side before you cut. Weight the template and cut out the pattern piece with your rotary cutter. Staystitch.

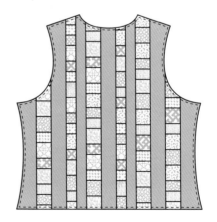

Moving On

To complete your vest, refer to "Part VI: The Lining" on pages 61–71 and "Part VII: Finishing" on pages 72–75.

PART V
The Statement Vest

Statement Vest

The Statement Vest is an easy-fitting, finger-tip-length garment. It features asymmetrical patchwork yokes on the front and back. A coordinating right collar is caught in the shoulder seam and attached to the front edge with binding. The vest also features deep pockets hidden in the side front seams. Wear this figure-flattering vest as a sleeveless jacket over dresses or with tops and pants.

You will create the pieced yokes and apply them to the garment pieces like appliqué, then construct the collar and finish with bias binding.

You can use any of the piecing techniques shown for the Weskits to make the patchwork for the yokes and collar. Choose the technique you want to use, do the piecing and make the yokes and collar, then construct the vest. Of course, you can also create your own variations. Sometimes I cut plain yokes and add only a bit of patchwork along the lower edges, for example.

Materials: 44"-wide fabric

2 yds. fashion fabric for the vest fronts and back
¾ yd. contrasting solid or print for the binding
12 to 15 fat quarters (18" x 22") of coordinating
    fabrics for the yokes and collar
2 yds. cotton fabric for the lining
Thread in a coordinating or neutral color
Statement Vest pattern pieces

Cutting

1. Complete steps 1–5 of "Preparing for Your Project" on page 15.

 Note

For this vest, it is not necessary to make poster-board templates for the front and back. Simply trace the front and back patterns for your size from the master pattern onto a piece of tracing paper or pattern-tracing cloth. Do, however, make templates for the front and back yokes and the collar.

2. From the fashion fabric, cut 2 vest fronts, 2 side fronts, 1 back, and 1 collar. Chalk-mark all notches and set aside.
3. See page 63 for cutting the vest lining and pockets.

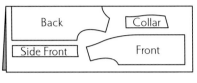

Cut 1.

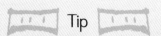
Tip

If your lining fabric is a contrasting color, cut the pockets from a fabric that matches the fashion fabric so flashy pockets don't peek out at the side seams.

Making the Yokes and Collar

1. Look through "Part II: The Vest Fronts" on pages 17–35 and select the piecing technique you want to use for your Statement Vest.
2. Following the directions for the chosen technique, make enough patchwork for the front and back yokes. Next, look at the collars in the photos below and note that since they are relatively small in comparison to the yokes, the patchwork was scaled down. (Large patches would lose definition in the narrow collar.) Press the completed patchwork blanks and cut out, using the poster-board pattern templates and a rotary cutter.

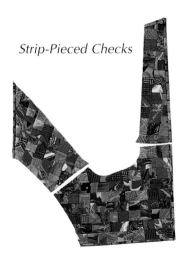

Solid with Strip-Pieced Checks

Strips and Strings

Crazy Pieced

Strip-Pieced Checks

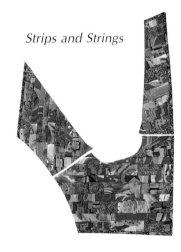

Crazy Cabin

Stack-and-Whack

3. Select a fabric to bind the yokes and collar. I rarely use the same fabric for these pieces as I use to bind the vest. To bind the yokes, cut a 2"-wide strip, or use one of your leftover strips. (This does not need to be a bias strip since the yoke edges have no curves.) Next, cut a 2½"-wide strip long enough to bind the collar edges and set it aside.

4. With right sides together, sew a 2"-wide strip to the bottom edge of the front yoke, using a ⅜"-wide seam allowance. Press the binding toward the seam allowance.

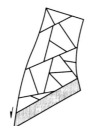

5. Fold the strip to the underside of the front yoke, over the seam allowance, and press. Pin in place or fuse to the yoke underside with a narrow strip of fusible web.

6. To sew a 2"-binding strip to the lower and side edges of the back yoke, begin at one end and stitch to the opposite end, ending the stitching ⅜" from the edge. Backstitch and clip the threads.

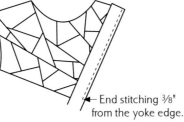

← End stitching ⅜" from the yoke edge.

7. Remove the yoke from the sewing machine and turn it counterclockwise. Fold the binding strip up and away from the top edge, forming a 45°-angle fold.

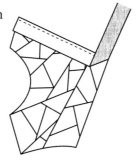

8. Hold the fold in place with your finger and bring the binding strip straight down along the yoke with raw edges even. There will be a fold along the top edge of the binding, even with the top edge of the yoke. Pin the strip in place and stitch ⅜" from the raw edges. Trim the excess binding even with the edge of the yoke.

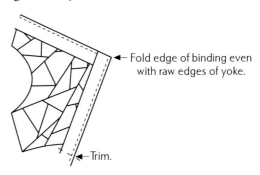

← Fold edge of binding even with raw edges of yoke.

←Trim.

9. Turn the binding toward the seam allowance and press. A mitered fold will form at the corner. Turn the strip to the underside of the yoke, over the seam allowance, and press. Pin or fuse as you did for the front yoke.

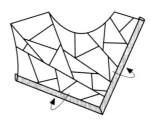

10. With wrong sides together, pin the patchwork collar to the fashion fabric collar. Baste a scant ¼" from all raw edges.

11. To bind the collar edge, fold the 2½"-wide binding strip in half lengthwise, wrong sides together. Press. Bind the outer edges of the collar following the directions for "Attaching the Binding" on pages 74–75, and miter the corner as shown in steps 7–9 above. Stitch in-the-ditch of the binding seam, catching the underside of the binding to the collar.

Stitch in-the-ditch.

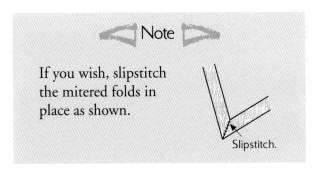

Note

If you wish, slipstitch the mitered folds in place as shown.

Slipstitch.

Assembling the Vest Shell

1. Arrange the vest fronts and side fronts face up on your work surface. With right sides together, pin and stitch a pocket piece (see page 63) to the lower edge of each vest front and side front, noting that the pockets extend 1" below the bottom edge of each. (You will trim the excess later.) Use a ¼"-wide seam allowance and sew from the top edge of the pocket to the bottom edge of each vest and side front. Press the pocket toward the seam allowance; edgestitch through all layers for added stability.

2. With right sides together, stitch each side front/pocket to a vest front/pocket as shown, using a ½"-wide seam allowance. Measure 6" down from the upper pocket corner and mark with a pin. Stitch from the pin to the bottom edge of the vest front, ⅛" inside the pocket stitching line.

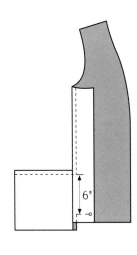

6"

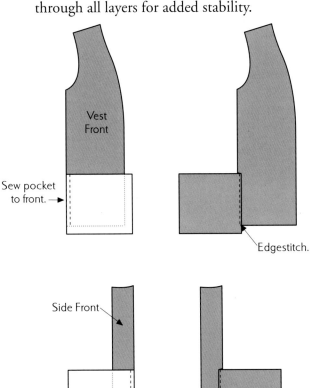

Vest Front

Sew pocket to front. →

Edgestitch.

Side Front

Edgestitch.

3. Press the seam and pocket toward the vest front. Pin the pocket in place and stitch through all layers, a scant ¼" from the vest-front raw edge. Trim excess pocket even with the front edge. *Do not trim the excess at the bottom edge yet.*

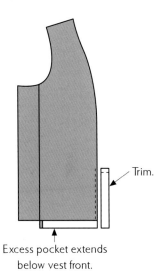

Trim.

Excess pocket extends below vest front.

4. Place the front yoke on the left vest front and pin in place with neck and shoulder edges even. Stitch a scant ¼" from the armhole, shoulder, and neckline edges. *Leave the bottom edge of the yoke loose for now.*

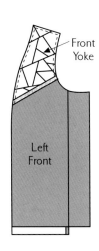

Front Yoke

Left Front

5. Pin the collar to the neckline and shoulder edges of the right vest front. Stitch a scant ¼" from the shoulder and front raw edges.

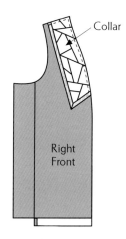

6. Place the vest back right side up on your work surface and press to remove any wrinkles. Pin the back yoke to the vest back with neck, shoulder, and left armhole edges even. Stitch a scant ¼" from the raw edges. Leave the bottom edge loose for now.

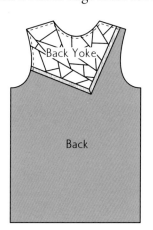

Adding Extra Bits

If you think the fronts and back look bare after attaching the patchwork pieces, you can tuck extra bits—small dimensional embellishments such as Prairie Points or knots—under the loose bottom edges of the pieces before stitching them in place. The decision to add an extra bit is entirely personal. I audition embellishments to see what works best.

Prairie Points

1. Cut 4" squares from several of the fabrics you used for the yokes and collar.
2. Fold each square in half and press.
3. Cut a ½" x 1½" strip of paper-backed fusible web; apply along the raw edge.

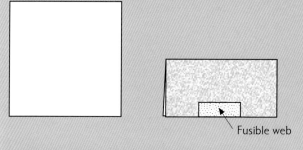

4. Remove the paper backing from the fusible web. Turn down 1 folded corner so the side raw edges are even with the bottom raw edges; fuse. Repeat with the other corner.

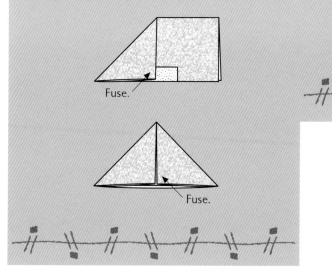

Knots

1. Cut 1½" x 6" strips from several of the fabrics you used for the yokes and collar. Fold each strip in half lengthwise, right sides together, and sew a scant ¼" from the raw edges, backstitching at each end. Turn each tube right side out, and press with the seam along one long edge.

2. Tie an overhand knot at one end of the tube, leaving a tail approximately 1" long. Pull the knot tight and manipulate so the end lies flat. Trim the tail at an angle and treat the cut edge with a thin bead of seam sealant, such as FrayCheck, to prevent raveling.

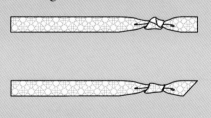

Finishing the Yokes

1. Audition Prairie Points or knots along the lower edges of the front and back yokes. When satisfied with their arrangement, pin them in place and pin the yoke on top of them. Make sure the additions are tucked far enough past the binding stitching line that they will be caught in the stitching.

2. Stitch in-the-ditch along the yoke binding stitching, catching the Prairie Points or knots in the seam.

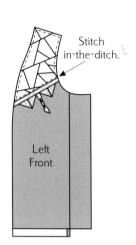

Stitch in-the-ditch.

Right Front

Left Front

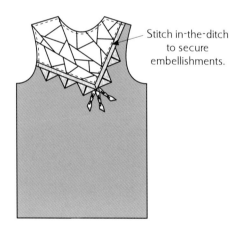

Stitch in-the-ditch to secure embellishments.

3. With right sides together and raw edges even, stitch the vest fronts to the vest back at the shoulders and side seams, using ½"-wide seam allowances. Backstitch at the beginning and end of each seam.

4. Staystitch ⅛" from the front edges to prevent stretching. Place the completed garment on a hanger where you can see it while you make and embellish the lining. (See pages 61–71.)

PART VI
The
Lining

Assembling the Vest

Before you begin the lining, complete the vest assembly.

1. With right sides together, stitch the vest fronts to the back at the shoulder seams (and the side seams for the Weskit) using ½"-wide seam allowances. Press seams open.

2. Turn the vest right side out and hang on a hanger close to your work area, referring to it as you design and complete your lining.

Preparing the Pieces for Embellishment

Now you are ready to prepare the lining and play with fabric paint. First, select a lining fabric in a color that blends with the vest. Since the patchwork contains several colors, you will have several choices. Choose a color that enhances the vest's wearability. For example, if there is orange in the vest but orange doesn't go with anything else you own, don't make the lining orange.

Materials: 44"-wide cotton fabric

Weskit: 1½ yds.
Statement Vest: 2 yds.

Cutting

1. Press the lining fabric and fold lengthwise with selvages even.
2. From paper, make 2 pocket patterns, each 12" x 13".
3. Position the pattern pieces as shown, allowing an extra 1" below the bottom edge of the back pattern piece.
4. Cut out the pieces, adding 1" to the bottom edge of the lining back. The extra length ensures that the lining and vest will fit together perfectly. Sometimes the patchwork vest relaxes and lengthens while it hangs waiting for the lining. (This happens occasionally when I have been overzealous with the steam iron.) You will remove any excess length later in the construction process.

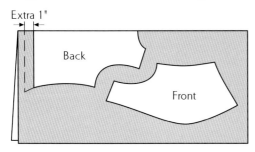

Weskit

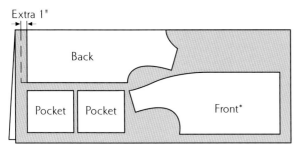

Statement Vest

For the Statement Vest, refer to the pattern sheet for front lining cutting directions.

5. Carefully press out the center fold in the vest back.
6. For the Weskit only, place the 3 lining pieces side by side on a prepared painting surface. (See "Getting Ready" on pages 68–69.) Be careful not to stretch the cut edges as you handle them.

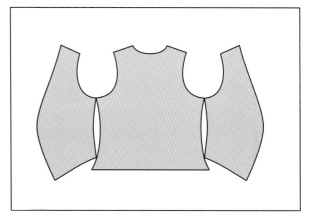

Weskit ready for embellishing

7. Continue with the following steps for the lining of the Statement Vest only.

    With right sides together, sew the lining fronts to the lining back at the sides, using a ½"-wide seam allowance. Backstitch at the beginning and end of each seam. The back piece will extend 1" below the bottom edges of the fronts.
8. Press the seams open and arrange the vest lining on your prepared painting surface. (See "Getting Ready" on pages 68–69.)

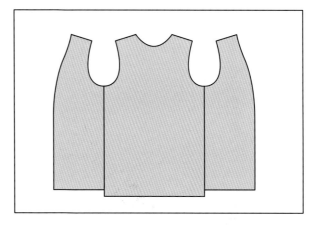

Statement Vest ready for embellishing

Designing the Embellishments

Embellishing the lining is the fun part of making a vest. It's where I allow wit and whimsy to take over. I try not to spend too much time planning the design. Instead, I listen to the happy (and sometimes silly) voice in my head—the one that says in a conspiratorial tone, "Go ahead, try it. I want to see what it will look like."

Look at the linings of the vests shown in this book. They may be similar in pattern, but each has its own personality. If you are stuck for ideas, gather your doodles. There's bound to be an idea there. Most of my doodles are geometric figures—triangles, circles, squares, dots—the ones you see scattered on the pages of this book. If yours are more realistic—boats, cats, bugs, for example—consider making a simple stencil of one (or more) of your favorites.

To get started, hang the completed vest shell near your work area where you can refer to it often. It will probably suggest to you the design to stamp or stencil on the lining. Vest shells often speak to me about what the lining should look like. Some color and pattern combinations cry out for a particular stencil or group of stencil designs; some require what I call a "circuit board" pattern—one that I paint freehand using a plastic squeeze bottle with a fine-tip applicator. Some need a serpentine line of triangles, dots, and squiggles.

Designing Stencils and Sponge Stamps

With a stencil, you can repeat a hard-edged design over and over on your lining. Use anything for the design; you don't have to be an artist to produce wonderful results. Try some of the following ideas.

◇ Borrow from other media. Look through your junk mail for small designs. Print advertising is another excellent source. Small motifs often appear in newspaper and magazine ads. Clip those that appeal to you and file them for later use. I have even traced designs from bathroom floors!

◇ I enjoy using animals in my quilts and linings. Origami books are an invaluable source of animal shapes for stencils. Dover Publications offers books with a vast assortment of patterns that can be used without securing permission from the publisher. Do be aware that *copyrights protect most designs in books and periodicals*, so be careful not to use an image from these sources unless you adapt it. (See "Mail-Order Sources" on page 78.)

Once you've chosen an image from a printed source, use a photocopy machine with reduction and enlargement capability to scale the image up or down for your needs. Or if you prefer, use the grid method of adapting a design.

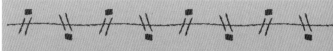

Adapting a Design on a Grid

The grid method does not make exact copies, but the resulting design will have more personality than a photocopy.

1. Trace the design onto plain paper.
2. Measure the design at its widest point. Using that measurement, draw a square around the design, making sure it touches the design on both sides at the widest point.
3. Cut out the design on the lines of the square. Cut a second square the desired size of the finished design.

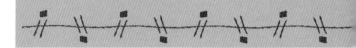

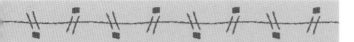

4. Using a ruler and a pencil, draw a 16-square grid over the design and on the empty square.

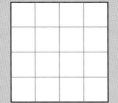

5. Look carefully at the divisions on both grids. Place pencil dots on the empty square where design lines cross grid lines. It is easiest to start in one corner and work your away across the design and the empty grid from square to square. If there are several lines within one grid square, subdivide that square into 4 squares to make it easier to transfer the design.

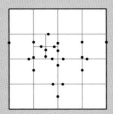

6. Using a pencil, connect the dots to form the design. Check the new design against the original and erase and redraw if you need to—but don't be too critical. Your new design should have its own personality.

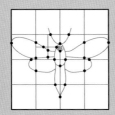

◇ Use natural materials as a design source. Flowers and leaves are perfect. Collect leaves and flowers, then press them between the pages of a discarded magazine. You can reduce or enlarge them on a photocopy machine as well. Pay attention to the vein lines in leaves. They will be the bridges when you draft and cut your stencil pattern (page 66).
◇ Don't forget geometric shapes. Group related shapes of various sizes to create new designs.

Making Sponge Stamps

Stamps cut from sponges create images with soft edges. It's fun to play with the variety of sponges available. Each has its own personality, and the resulting images are unique. Cut stamps from a household sponge that has a stiff plastic scrubber on one side, using the scrubber as a handle. Other foam sponges are also appropriate; each type offers different paint coverage and results. Upholstery foam has a fine grain and makes shapes with even coverage. Compressed sponges work best for cutting complex shapes. Be sure to rinse new sponges before cutting shapes and applying paint. (The antibacterial solution on new sponges rejects paint.)

To get an accurate stamp shape, experiment with scissors and a craft knife, since each cuts a bit differently. Since the shapes I use are simple, I use paper scissors for compressed sponges and household sponges with a scrubber backing. I either cut the design freehand or draw it on the sponge with a fine-point permanent marker, and then cut it out with scissors.

Making Stencils

Look at the motif(s) you have chosen for your stencils and determine which areas to cut out and where the bridges, if needed, will be. Bridges are narrow connectors that hold the design together. They block the paint, leaving areas unprinted. Lay tracing paper over the motif to try out your ideas for cutting the stencil.

Examine the development of a stencil from this picture of a lizard. I used tracing paper and pencil to transform the original into one that works well as a stencil. The lizard needed to be flattened and the various design elements isolated. For example, the bulbous toes would have been difficult to cut, so I eliminated them from the stencil, adding paint-dot toes to the final design.

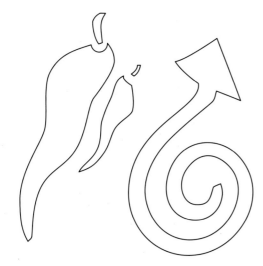

Stencils without bridges

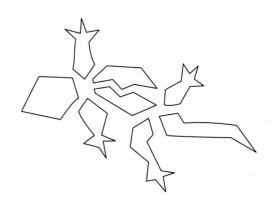

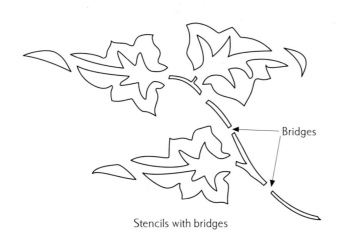

Bridges

Stencils with bridges

Materials

Permanent, extra-fine tip pen
Sheet of .003mm or .005mm clear or smoke-
colored acetate (Quilting-template plastic is
too thick. Paint tends to crawl under the
edges, creating blurred designs.)
Self-healing rotary-cutting mat
Craft knife with a new #11 blade
Transparent tape

Directions

1. Using the marking pen, trace your final design onto the acetate sheet.

    Working on the rotary-cutting mat and
using the craft knife, cut out the inner areas
of the stencil as your design requires. Leave
bridges where needed to hold the design together. Begin cutting in the center of the design to retain maximum strength of the
acetate as you maneuver. For the same rea-
son, cut out the smaller shapes first. Move
the acetate so you are always drawing the
knife toward you. If your design is direc-
tional and you want to print mirror images,
make another stencil. Using both sides of
the same stencil is too messy.

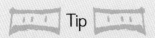
Tip

If you make a cutting mistake, carefully
mend the cut with transparent tape,
then trim the tape that extends into the
cutout areas.

Applying the Embellishments

Materials

Prepared stencil(s) and/or sponge stamps
Plastic squeeze bottles with fine-tip applicators.
You will need 1 bottle for each color of
paint you use. Your local craft store may
carry these, or refer to the list of mail-order
sources on page 78.
Large, plastic drop cloth
Apron and old clothes. I prefer a chef's apron
large enough to wrap to the back since I
usually wipe my hands in the hip area.
Rubber or latex gloves. The paint I use washes
off, but if you have sensitive skin or a beautiful manicure, protect yourself with gloves.
Chalk pencil
Water-soluble *opaque* fabric paints. I use
Neopaque™ and Lumiere™. They offer the
best coverage and opacity. That's important
to me because I use dark and intense colors
for the lining, and translucent paints do not
show up well. Refer to the list of mail-order
sources on page 78.
Large hat pin or needle. Use this to clear the
gunk from the applicator tips of the paint
bottles. A straightened paper clip works too.
Smooth, flat trays or plates. Use these for your
paint palette. I prefer trays. It's easier to
scrape excess paint from them back into the
paint bottle. Meat and microwave meals are
often packaged on foam trays that also
work well.
Several 1"-wide sponge brushes. Called trim
brushes in hardware stores; the best ones
have wooden handles.
Several sponge daubers. Refer to the directions
in the box on page 68 to make your own.

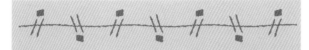

Making a Sponge Dauber

Make several daubers so you don't have to clean them to switch paint colors. (I learned how to make daubers from the late Lenore Davis in her painting and stamping workshop.)

1. Cut a 3" square and a 6"-diameter circle from a ¼"-thick sponge.
2. Fold the square in half, then in half again. Wrap the circle around the folded square, then secure with a tightly wrapped rubber band. If you want a handle, add a 2"- to 3"-long piece of ½"- to ¾"-diameter dowel before securing the rubber band.

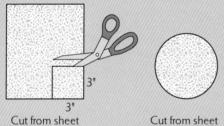

Cut from sheet of ¼"-thick sponge.

Cut from sheet of ¼"-thick sponge.

Fold into small square.

Place folded square in center of circle.

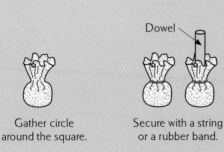

Gather circle around the square.

Secure with a string or a rubber band.

Wide-mouthed quart jar. Use a jar or a clean yogurt container filled with water for clean up.

Paper towels

Cotton-tipped swabs. I use these to produce soft-edged dots.

Gold or silver fine-point permanent fabric marker. Use a metallic marker to sign your name on the lining.

As you gather these materials, be on the lookout for other items that might make an interesting pattern or design when dipped in paint and stamped on fabric. I print one of my favorite spiral patterns using a napkin ring I bought at an import store. I also use nuts (as in nuts and bolts) in a variety of sizes.

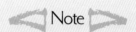

If you use a piece of kitchen equipment even once for painting or dyeing, *never* return it to kitchen use. If paints and dyes were intended to be eaten, they would be flavored and have nutrition labels. In fact, some dyes are poisonous and others are carcinogenic. Get into the habit of keeping your studio equipment separate from your kitchen equipment. Mark studio equipment with a permanent marker and store it away from the kitchen.

Getting Ready

You are about to begin applying paint to your lining. Gather all the supplies listed above before you begin, and remove anything from your work area that could get splattered with undesired paint.

1. Cover the work surface with a plastic drop cloth and smooth out any folds or wrinkles. Put on old clothes. (Your fingers are sure to get smeared with paint. If you're anything at all like me, you will wipe your hands on your clothes—without thinking.) Put on an apron too.

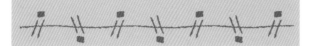

2. Read the instructions that come with the paint you will be using. Some paints require curing and have special cleaning requirements. If the paint is not labeled "dry cleanable," paint a sample design on a lining fabric scrap, follow the curing and heat setting directions, then ask the dry cleaner to clean it for you. Most dry cleaners are willing to do this, especially if you ask them to run it in their last batch of solution and explain what type of paint it is. (They might fear that the paint will melt and gum up their cleaning solution, not to mention anything that's in the solution. Sparkle paints sold for painting sweatshirts and decorating appliqués are not dry cleanable; they melt and disappear into the dry-cleaning solution.

3. Practice. If you are nervous about committing paint to fabric, it's a good idea to make some samples with the various tools you have collected. Think about how the shapes work together. If you are still unsure, continue practicing on paper—butcher paper or newsprint. Draw the vest-front shapes on the paper, and try out your design ideas. When you are comfortable with the process described below, you're ready to take the next step.

Stamping and Stenciling Preliminaries

1. Arrange the lining pieces on the drop cloth–covered surface, butting together side edges if making the Weskit. (If making the Statement Vest, the side seams should be stitched and pressed already.) Arranging the pieces this way allows you to connect the front and back designs so they are continuous and interrelated. This is called an "engineered" design because the design fits the specific garment shape, unlike a preprinted fabric, which has a design that extends from selvage to selvage.

2. Using a chalk pencil, draw a serpentine line on your lining. Make a bold, flowing line that fills the lining. If you use circles, make them fairly large because you will fill them with design motifs. Don't worry if you don't like the first lines. Rub them out with a *slightly damp* sponge and start again. If the fabric is wet, allow it to dry before drawing, since chalk may leave a stain if used on wet areas.

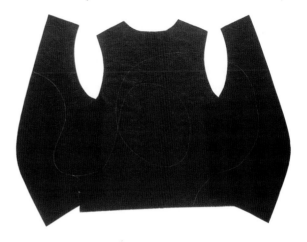

3. Pour a small amount of each paint into separate trays. Pour only those colors you plan to use right away, since the paint will begin to dry as soon as you pour it.

Note

I use the paint right out of the bottle without diluting it, and I rarely mix paints to get a new color. Paint should have the consistency of partially solidified pudding. The more fluid it is, the more difficult it is to control, especially when working with stencils.

Stamping with Sponges

1. Dab the shape into the paint so the entire stamping surface is coated.
2. Position the paint-filled surface on the lining along the chalk line and press down firmly. You should be able to make 2 or 3 printed impressions with one load of paint.

3. Continue making impressions along the line in the desired locations.

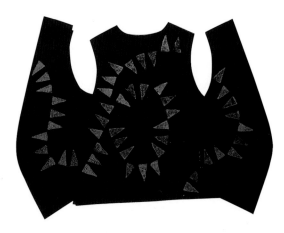

4. If you wish, use other implements in the same way as the sponge. In the vest shown, I used my favorite napkin ring to add the triangular-shaped spirals.

5. Add dots if desired, using a plastic squeeze bottle with a fine-tip applicator.

Stenciling

1. Place the stencil in position along the chalked line and hold it flat and still with one hand.
2. Dip a sponge brush or sponge dauber (page 68) into the fabric paint and wipe off excess.
3. Evenly press the brush or dauber all over the stencil, making sure the paint covers all cut-out areas. Do not rub or scrub over the surface of the stencil as you risk forcing unwanted paint under the stencil edges. (Sometimes this makes a charming shape irregularity, but usually it makes an ugly blotch.)

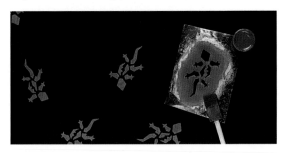

4. Carefully lift the stencil from the surface of the fabric. Wipe away any paint that may have crawled under the stencil edges.
5. If you want to print other shapes over the first ones, allow the paint to dry for about 30 minutes—even longer if the weather is humid. You don't want the images to smear when you overprint with a new shape and/or color.

6. To finish the design, add dots and squiggles in a regular pattern along the serpentine chalk line (See "Other Printing Methods"

below.) Or try adding freehand squares or triangles as in the Weskit shown. You may also want to add dots and squiggles in open, undecorated areas of the lining. Be cautious, however. If it feels like one more may be one too many, it probably is. It's better for the finished design to have some open spaces than to have too many images, making the finished lining look crowded.

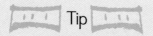 Tip

Whether you are stamping with a sponge or other device or using stencils, it is important to evaluate your work as you go. Stand back and examine the work in progress. Look for unbalanced areas of the design. Are there spaces that are too blank? Can you add a printed shape or group of shapes to fill in? A rhythmic pattern of shapes stenciled above and below the chalk line is pleasing and fun. Remember that you are doing hand work. The irregularity of the marks you make adds to the character of the finished piece. Enjoy the process.

Other Printing Methods

To use squeeze bottles to make dots or squiggles, cut off the applicator tip to make a hole. Be conservative. Cut off a small amount of the tip and test by drawing a line of paint. Make some test dots too. If the line or the dots are too small, cut off a bit more and try again.

While using the squeeze bottle, shake it often to keep the paint flowing. Use a long hat pin, needle, or paper clip to unclog the tip if a glob of paint forms there.

Keep bottles tightly capped when not in use. The paint dries out fairly quickly, forming lumps that clog the tip.

When stamping with hard objects, be careful not to overload the surface. When you stamp with too much paint, it can run or obscure the shape you are trying to make. Practice on fabric scraps to determine how much paint is enough for the fabric and paint you are using.

Cleaning Up

1. Return any unused paint to its bottle and wash out sponges and brushes immediately so you can use them again. (They will be ruined if you allow the paint to dry in them.) If you must wait to wash them, put them in the container of water to soak.
2. Wash the paint trays and put them away to use again.

Setting the Paint

1. Allow the painted lining to dry completely—at least 4 hours, or overnight if possible. Make sure all thick dots are completely dry. They will look like a dome has collapsed when dry and should not feel the least bit squishy when you touch them with *gentle* pressure.
2. Follow the directions on the paint container for setting the paint to make it permanent. This usually means ironing the painted surface for 30 seconds to 2 minutes with the iron set at the highest setting appropriate for the fabric. I use the cotton setting and a lightweight press cloth. The cloth protects the iron sole plate from not-quite-dry areas. You can use a flat-bed presser if you have one, but be sure to use a press cloth.

PART VII
Finishing

You're ready to complete your one-of-a-kind vest. Follow the directions below for the Weskit or Statement Vest.

Assembling the Lining

All seam allowances are ½" wide.

1. With right sides together, stitch the vest-front lining pieces to the back at the shoulders (and at the side seams for the Weskit). Backstitch at the beginning and end of each seam. Press the seams open.

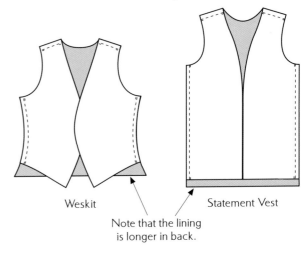

Weskit   Statement Vest

Note that the lining is longer in back.

2. Place the lining inside the vest, *wrong sides together*. Carefully match the shoulder and side seams, and pin securely. Pin all edges together except the back bottom edge. Machine baste a scant ¼" from all pinned edges, removing the pins as you go for ease of handling.

3. Hang the garment while you prepare the binding. The patchwork vest may relax and grow as much as ½" during this period. If you pin, trim, and finish the vest without letting it hang, the lining may be too short and the lower back edge will pull up inside after you have worn it for awhile.

Preparing the Binding

Now is the time to choose a binding to finish the vest edges. As you choose the binding fabric, think about it as an outline for the vest edges. If you choose a contrasting fabric, it will make a strong visual impact. Matching or low-contrast fabric will almost disappear. To see this effect, examine the photos of the vests in this book. Notice the strong vertical lines along the front edges when a contrasting binding was used to finish them.

There are three binding options: cut the binding from a single solid-colored fashion fabric such as silk noil, cut it from a print fabric, or piece it from more than one fabric.

Pieced Bias Binding

1. Choose 2 to 4 patterned fabrics; you can use leftovers from the vest patchwork. Fold them so they are about 5" to 6" wide and lay them side by side to see what they will look like when cut and pieced together. To see what they will look like on the bias, place a 3"-wide paper window across them on the diagonal. If you wish, you can vary the width of the fabrics for a different look.

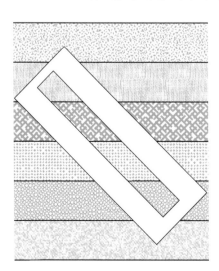

Use a window template placed on the diagonal to evaluate fabrics.

2. From each fabric, cut a selvage-to-selvage strip the width you determined in step 1. I usually cut 5"-wide strips, but I cut wider strips when using Japanese yukata cloth.

3. Sew the strips together along the long edges, using a ¼"-wide seam allowance. Press all seams in one direction.

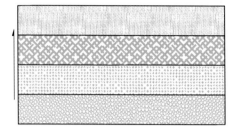

4. Fold down one corner to find the true bias and press lightly, or use the 45°-angle line on your rotary ruler to locate the bias.

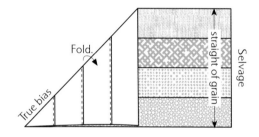

5. Cut along the fold line, then cut 2½"-wide bias strips using the rotary cutter, ruler, and mat. You need enough strips to make approximately 5 yards of binding for the Weskit or 6 yards of binding for the Statement Vest.

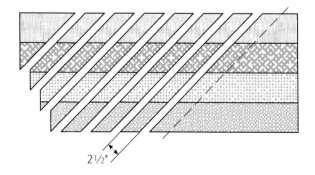

6. Stitch the strips together as shown to make one continuous strip of binding. Press the seams open and trim the ears that extend beyond the strip edges.

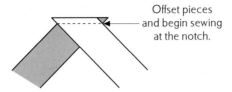

Offset pieces and begin sewing at the notch.

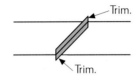

Trim.

Trim.

7. Fold the strip in half lengthwise, wrong sides together, and press lightly, taking care not to stretch the binding.

Single-Fabric Bias Binding

If you plan to use a single fabric for the binding, you will need ½ yard of 44"-wide fabric. To cut and prepare it for the vest, follow steps 4–6 of the directions for "Pieced Bias Binding" starting on page 73.

Attaching the Binding

Do not trim the excess lining fabric at the bottom edge of the vest back until instructed to do so.

1. Beginning at the bottom edge of the vest front, pin the binding to the garment, right sides together and raw edges even. End at the bottom edge of the other vest front.

2. Stitch ¼" from the raw edges, backstitching at the beginning and end of the seam.

Right side of vest

3. To bind the armholes, first open the end of the binding and turn under the raw edge at a 45° angle. Trim ¼" from the fold. Refold the bias strip.

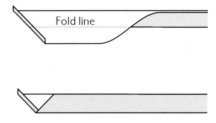

Fold line

4. Beginning close to the underarm seam, pin the binding to the armhole, right sides together and raw edges even. When you reach the starting point, cut the bias strip just long enough to tuck under the folded end. Stitch ¼" from the raw edges, overlapping the stitching where it meets.

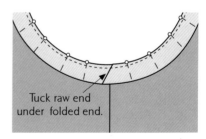

Tuck raw end under folded end.

5. Press all binding toward the seam allowance, being careful not to stretch it.

6. Turn the folded edge of the binding to the inside of the vest, over the seam allowance, with the folded edge just covering the stitching. Pin in place, then slipstitch on the inside or stitch in-the-ditch on the outside. Take extra care with this step so you can reverse your vest and wear it lining-side out.

 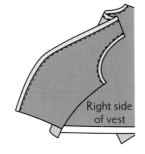

Slipstitch on the inside.   OR   Stitch in-the-ditch.

7. You're almost finished, and you deserve a break! Give yourself a pat on the back and place the vest on a hanger to relax while you have a cup of tea. Then finish the bottom edges of the vest front and back (steps 8–11).

8. While you relaxed, so did the vest. Now it's time to adjust the back bottom edge. Pin the front bottom edges together, then pin the vest back to the lining, matching the side seams.

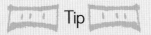 Tip

For the best fit, pin the bottom edges together while the vest is on a hanger.

9. With an extra 1" extending at the front bottom edge as shown above right, pin the binding to the vest, right sides together and raw edges of the binding even with the raw edges of the vest. Allow a 1½"-long tail of binding at the other front edge as well.

Stitch ¼" from the raw edges, backstitching as you begin and end.

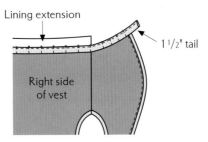

10. Remove the pins and trim the lining even with the bottom edge of the vest. On the Statement Vest, trim away the excess pocket that extends below the vest-front bottom edge.

11. Trim the excess binding ¼" from the vest-front edges. Press and turn the binding as you did for the front and armhole edges, turning in the raw edge at each front edge. Sew in place by hand or machine.

The Finishing Touch

Sign and date your creation, using a permanent marking pen. I usually sign the left front lining at the bottom. If you have your own label, sew it in with pride. Mine goes at the left armhole so it is not noticeable if the vest is worn lining-side out.

Last, but certainly most important, put on your new vest and strut your stuff. I know you will enjoy wearing it for years to come, and you'll want to get started on the next one right away.

Appendix

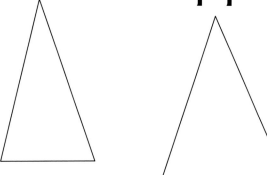

Stencil and Stamp Patterns

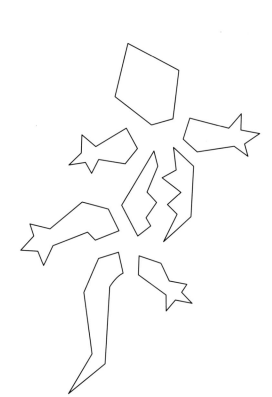

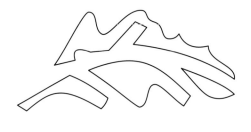

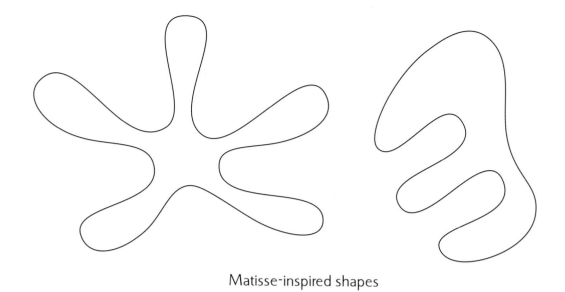

Matisse-inspired shapes

Origami-inspired animals

Mail-Order Sources

Clotilde, Inc.
2 Sew Smart Way, B8031, Stevens Point, WI 54481-8031; 800-772-2891. This mail-order company carries sewing notions and fine-tip squeeze bottles for fabric paints.

Dharma Trading Co.
PO Box 150916, San Rafael, CA 94915; 800-542-5227. Dharma carries fabric paints and tools, including brushes and plastic squeeze bottles.

Dover Publications, Inc.
Dept. 23, 31 East Second Street, Mineola, NY, 11501. Dover publishes books of copy-right-free designs and patterns. Many are available at your local bookstore.

Rupert, Gibbon, and Spider, Inc.
PO Box 425, Healdsburg, CA 98448; 800-442-0455. This company carries fabric paints and tools, and is the exclusive supplier of Neopaque™ and Lumiere™.

Sax Arts and Crafts
PO Box 510710, New Berlin, WI 53151; 800-558-6696. Sax carries general art supplies and some fabric paints.

Thai Silks
252 (T) State Street, Los Altos, CA 94022; 800-722-SILK or 800-221-SILK in California. Thai Silks carries raw silk by the yard in many colors as well as other natural-fiber fabrics, including other silks, woolens, and some cottons.

Bibliography

Birren, Faber. *Principles of Color*. New York: Van Nostrand Reinhold Company, 1969.

Hammond, Suzanne Tessier. *Designing Quilts: The Value of Value*. Bothell, Wash.: That Patchwork Place, 1993.

Horton, Roberta. *The Fabric Makes the Quilt*. Lafayette, Calif.: C & T Publishing, 1995.

Itten, Johannes. *The Elements of Color*. New York: Van Nostrand Reinhold Company, 1970.

Laury, Jean Ray. *Imagery on Fabric*. Lafayette, Calif.: C & T Publishing, 1992.

Murrah, Judy. *Jacket Jazz*. Bothell, Wash.: That Patchwork Place, 1993.

Murrah, Judy. *Jacket Jazz Encore*. Bothell, Wash.: That Patchwork Place, 1994.

Robinson, Lynne and Richard Lowther. *Stenciling*. North Pomfret, Vt.: Trafalgar Square Publishing, 1995.

Rozmyn, Mia. *Freedom in Design: New Directions in Foundation Paper Piecing*. Bothell, Wash.: That Patchwork Place, 1995.

About the Author

Charlotte Soeters Bird is a talented designer of one-of-a-kind artwear. The idea for Birdworks (the name of Charlotte's business) was born in a one-room cabin in Alaska where Charlotte had gone with her husband, Charlie, for a sabbatical. After thirteen years of government work, her creative soul longed for expression. Armed with a treadle sewing machine, a quilt frame, and five boxes of fabric, Charlotte escaped the hustle and bustle of urban life and focused on developing her design sense. Not surprisingly, she left her job and now lives in San Diego, California, where she works in a studio overlooking the bay.

Charlotte's work has been displayed in juried shows around the country, including the wearables show sponsored by the American Crafts Museum in New York City, the Bazaar del Mundo Fabric Fantasies Festival in San Diego, and the L. Freud Crafts Gallery in Birmingham, Alabama. She also shows her work at juried crafts shows around the country. These venues include the American Crafts Enterprises Show in Baltimore, Maryland, the Contemporary Crafts Market in Santa Monica, California, and the Washington Crafts Expo in Washington, D. C. Charlotte's work is also featured in *Fiberarts Design Book IV* and *Ornament* magazine.

Charlotte also makes art quilts. She was a 1991 NICHE* finalist, and her work is included in numerous private and corporate collections.

NICHE is a national magazine published by the Rosen Group. NICHE awards are given annually in several craft categories, ranging from one-of-a-kind furniture to production clothing.

Publications and Products

Many titles are available at your local quilt shop.
For more information, write for a free color catalog
to That Patchwork Place, Inc., PO Box 118, Bothell,
WA 98041-0118 USA.

☎ U.S. and Canada, call **1-800-426-3126** for the
name and location of the quilt shop nearest you.
Int'l: 1-206-483-3313 **Fax:** 1-206-486-7596
E-mail: info@patchwork.com
Web: www.patchwork.com   12.96